THERE'S NO ONE LIKE
JESUS

THERE'S NO ONE LIKE
JESUS

BLAKE WESTERN

AMBASSADOR INTERNATIONAL
GREENVILLE, SOUTH CAROLINA & BELFAST, NORTHERN IRELAND

www.ambassador-international.com

There's No One like Jesus

ISBN: 978-1-62020-500-6
eISBN: 978-1-62020-403-0

Cover Design & Page Layout by Hannah Nichols
eBook Conversion by Anna Raats

AMBASSADOR INTERNATIONAL
Emerald House
427 Wade Hampton Blvd.
Greenville, SC 29609, USA
www.ambassador-international.com

AMBASSADOR BOOKS
The Mount
2 Woodstock Link
Belfast, BT6 8DD, Northern Ireland, UK
www.ambassadormedia.co.uk

The colophon is a trademark of Ambassador

CONTENTS

AFRICAN CHRISTIANS OFTEN SING A song in which they repeat these words over and over: "There's no one, there's no one like Jesus." And what they sing is true. There is no one like Jesus. He is far beyond our ability to describe. He is far beyond our capacity to fully comprehend. He is ever before us leading the way. He is ever behind us fulfilling all humanity's deepest desires. He is ever above us calling us to Himself.

If we look for the ideal man, we cannot look beyond Him. If we look for a God of love, we will come to Him. If we look for the most amazing person in history, we will point to Him. He is utterly unique. He is perfect God and perfect man in one person. He is the Lamb of God who takes away the sin of the world. He is the Good Shepherd who leads us to still waters. He is the Great Physician who heals the broken heart. He is the Light of the world for a world in darkness. He is the Water of Life for multitudes who are spiritually thirsty. He is the Bread of Life for the hungry of soul. He is the Life-Giver for all who are dead in trespasses and sins.

Jesus is all that anyone could ever hope for, all that anyone could ever desire, and all that we will ever need. He is everything we need today and forever. We will always need Him, follow Him, and rejoice in Him. "Christ is all and in all"

There has never been anyone like Jesus. There will never be anyone like Jesus. He is the King of Kings and the Lord of Lords. When we talk about Jesus, we exhaust all of the superlative words in a language. If we could bring together all the great preachers of the ages, they would tell us many wonderful things about Him. But we would know that all they could proclaim would only be a little of what is to be known about Him. If we could bring all the great choirs of the ages together to sing about His glories, when they were finished, we would still feel that the half had not been told. If we could bring all the great paintings of Jesus and put them into one, it might amaze us, but it would still be inadequate.

How can we tell of One who is the King of Kings and the Lord of Lords? How can we tell of One who conquered sin and death? How can we tell of the King in His beauty? How can we tell of One before whom Paul fell in blindness when His light was manifested? How can we tell of One before whom John fell as a dead man when he saw Christ in His glory? The answer is that we cannot do so adequately. However, there are many things we can say and sing that are true. And this we can always say: "There's no one, no one like Jesus."

This is how Samuel Rutherford spoke of Jesus: "This soul of ours hath love, and cannot but love some fair one. And oh what a fair One, what an only One, what an excellent, lovely, ravishing

One is Jesus! Put the beauty of ten thousand thousand worlds of paradises, like the garden of Eden in one; put all trees, all flowers, all smells, all colours, all tastes, all joys, all sweetness, all loveliness, in one: oh, what a fair and excellent thing would that be! And yet it would be less to that fair and dearest Well-beloved Christ, than one drop of rain to the whole seas, rivers, lakes, and fountains of ten thousand earths. Oh, but Christ is heaven's wonder and earth's wonder!"[1]

CHAPTER 1

THERE'S NO ONE LIKE JESUS IN HIS DEITY

BETHLEHEM WAS NOT THE BEGINNING of Jesus. He is the eternal Christ and has always existed. Bethlehem was the time in which He was born into this life. His humanity had a beginning. But in His deity, He has always existed. To understand something of the greatness of Christ, we must look to where He was before coming to this earth. In the Gospel of John 1:1, we read, "In the beginning was the Word, and the Word was with God, and the Word was God." In other words, before there was a universe, before there was a creation, there was the Trinity: the Father, Son, and Holy Spirit.

Our human minds cannot adequately understand the Trinity. How could a tiny ant understand a man or woman? Obviously, it could not. But the difference is far greater between a human being and God because ants and human beings are created beings. God is the Creator and we are part of the creation. So there will always be mysteries that we cannot grasp. When Jesus was baptized, the Spirit appeared in the form of a dove, and the Father spoke, "This is my Son, whom I love; with Him I am well pleased" (Matthew 3:17b). In the Great Commission, we are told to go and make disciples, "baptizing them in the name of the Father and of the Son and of the Holy Spirit" (Matthew 28:19b). It is not the plural "names," but the singular "name."

The explanation that Nathan Wood gives in a book entitled *The Secret of the Universe* is helpful. He says that when we talk about the Trinity, we do not add: 1 + 1 + 1 = 3. That would be *tritheism*, which means "three gods." In that way of thinking, each would be a separate god. This is what some people accuse Christians of believing. But this is not true. We believe in one God in three persons. Wood says that we should multiply when we talk about the Trinity: 1 x 1 x 1 = 1. Each member of the Trinity has all the attributes of the others, but there is only one God.

For instance, the Father is all-powerful. So is the Son Jesus Christ. It is also true of the Holy Spirit. The Father is present everywhere. The same is true of Christ and the Spirit. The Father is all-knowing. Likewise, the Son and the Spirit have all knowledge. The Father is eternal. So are Christ and the Spirit. Just as the Father is holy, so are Jesus and the Spirit.

There is no one like Jesus when we consider the Incarnation. Jesus, who existed from all eternity, became a tiny baby in a manger. This all happened without a human father. Jesus was born of the Virgin Mary through the work of the Holy Spirit. This was the explanation given to Mary in Luke 1:31–32: "You will be with child and give birth to a son, and you are to give Him the name Jesus. He will be great and will be called the Son of the Most High. The Lord God will give Him the throne of His father David." Mary did not understand, so the angel said, "The Holy Spirit will come upon you, and the power of the Most High will overshadow you. So the holy one to be born will be called the Son of God" (Luke 1:35).

Through the ages there have been skeptics who questioned the virgin birth. But it all fits in with the perfect, unique life of Jesus. It means that God has come down to man. Jesus did not cease to be God, but He took on human flesh and lived here. He was not pretending. He became a real man. He cried like other babies and drank milk like other babies. He looked like any other baby that you would meet. He learned like other children. The Bible says that He became poor that we could become rich (2 Corinthians 8:9). He left glory to bring us into His glory.

It is difficult for us to imagine the humiliation of Jesus in becoming a man. We live in a world where sin and death are everywhere, where pollution and destruction are with us. We live in a fallen world in rebellion against the very One who created it and became incarnate here. What would it mean for an honest and just person to be thrust into the worst prison imaginable? What would it mean for a prince living in a royal palace where he had everything at his command to move into a neighborhood where there was utter poverty and people searched through piles of garbage to find bits of food? For Jesus to come to this earth was a far greater humiliation.

Jesus left the place where there was perfect love to come to a place where there was hatred and fighting. Jesus left the place where there was wholeness and harmony to come to a place where there was sickness and dying. Jesus left the place of joy to come to a place of tears and sadness. Jesus left the place of light to come to a world of darkness and sin.

If you wanted to communicate with a miniscule ant and could become one and enter into their society, that would be a remarkable thing. But it would be nothing compared to Jesus leaving His glory to become a man. It is infinitely greater and beyond our ability to understand fully. But this is at the very center when we think about the uniqueness of Jesus. It is amazing. We must stand in awe, speechless before such majesty and love.

J. Sidlow Baxter said this about the incarnation: "The incarnation is the miracle-of-miracles, the meaning-of-meanings, which should rivet the attention of so-called Christendom today as never before. It is the fundamental interpretation of things, compared with which the splitting of the atom is a barely noticeable incident. As the angels of heaven look down upon this earthly scene, surely their biggest marvel must be the absence of human marvel at this eternal surprise – that infinity has clothed itself with our humanity."[2]

We must be clear. There are the two natures in the one person of Christ. He did not forsake His deity to become a man. And He did not leave His humanity when He ascended back into heaven. There was not a mixing of His humanity with His deity, as we would mix a cake. This helps us to understand many things that Jesus did on the earth. He prayed to the Father. Some would say, "How could He pray if He were God?" The answer is that He prayed as a man. Jesus's deity was veiled, so to speak, while He was on earth. Paul said that He emptied Himself: "Who, being in very nature God, did not consider equality with God something to be grasped, but made Himself nothing, taking the very nature of a servant, being made in human likeness" (Philippians 2:6–7).

Christ is fully God and He is fully man. Jesus took back to heaven something that He did not have when He came to earth: He took back a human body. His body did not vanish into noth-ingness. The Bible says that this same Jesus will come again. When the disciples saw Jesus after His resurrection, they saw the same person they had known and walked with for some three years. His humanity is forever joined to His deity. And today at the right hand of the Father, there is Jesus, both God and man in one person.

We must not deny either the deity or the humanity of Jesus. Charles H. Spurgeon said this: "He is as truly God as if He were not a man, and yet as completely and perfectly man as if He were not God."[3] Paul said, "For in Christ all the fullness of the Deity lives in bodily form" (Colossians 2:9). And Jesus startled the religious leaders of His day when He said, "Before Abraham was born, I am" (John 8:58b). Abraham had died hundreds of years before Jesus came to the earth. Jesus was actually using the name of God when He said, "I am." Moses had asked what God's name was and the Lord replied, "I am that I am." Jesus used that same name for Himself. I believe Jesus was doing the same when He said, "I am the way and the truth and the life" (John 14:6).

There is no one like Jesus. He is matchless and unique. He is Lord, the Son of God, the First and the Last, the Alpha and the Omega. He is God in the flesh, Emmanuel.

CHAPTER 2

THERE'S NO ONE LIKE JESUS IN HIS HUMANITY

IF WE TRY TO COMPARE Jesus to other men, He exceeds them all just as a blazing sun exceeds the light from a match. If we think of kings, then He is the King of Kings. If we compare Him to physicians, then He is the Great Physician. If we compare Him to Adam, He is the Second Adam. If we compare Him to other teachers, then He is the Master Teacher.

When we think of great men and women through the centuries, we can only say, "Jesus is beyond compare." He is greater than any one person and greater than all people put together. Jesus is the complete man. There is nothing lacking or unbalanced in Him. We cannot say that He needed more of this characteristic or more of that characteristic. He is the perfect man. We must not define humanity by looking at one another. We are the empty shells of a fallen humanity. Jesus is what God intended man to be.

How foolish it is to compare ourselves to other people. The only model is the perfect man, Jesus.

John Watson said this about Jesus: "No one has yet discovered the word Jesus ought to have said; none suggested that better word He might have said. No action of His has shocked our moral sense, none has fallen short of the ideal. He is full of surprises, but they are all the surprises of perfection."⁴ Dr. Charles Jefferson added these appropriate words about Jesus: "You can no more add anything to Him than you can add something to the sky. He pushed every good trait of human character to its utmost limit. His forgiveness was unbounded, His generosity was untiring, His patience was inexhaustible, His mercy was immeasurable, His courage was illimitable, His wisdom was unfathomable, His kindness was interminable, His faith removed mountains, His hope had no shadow in it, His love was infinite."⁵

The disciples who knew Jesus best were amazed at Him. They would be most likely to see any hypocrisy or weakness, but their testimony was unanimous. "He committed no sin, and no deceit was found in His mouth" (1 Peter 2:22). Who of us would dare ask the question that Jesus asked: "Can any of you prove me guilty of sin?" (John 8:46a). And no one could point to any failure or fault in Jesus. He is the only holy man who ever lived. He never had a sinful thought. He never said a sinful word. He never did a sinful deed.

The first man, Adam, fell in the face of temptation. Jesus also was tempted but He triumphed over the temptation. He refused to take the easy way to popularity. He refused to compromise the teaching of God's Word. Dr. R. G. Lee called Jesus "the great unlike." And that is an accurate description. Jesus is unique in His humanity.

It is a serious mistake to deny either the deity or the humanity of Jesus. He is both God and man in one person. Usually, heretical teaching errs on one side or the other. Some false teachers deny the deity of Christ. And that is unacceptable. Other false teachers deny the humanity of Jesus. And that is equally wrong and unacceptable. Both truths must be embraced and believed.

In history there have been many outstanding teachers. And we are indebted to their wisdom even today. Solomon was considered the wisest man in his day. He was well known for his proverbs and his knowledge. And yet there is a teacher who exceeds all other teachers, including Solomon. His name is Jesus. People who heard Jesus speak said, "No one ever spoke the way this man does" (John 7:46).

What was so unique about Jesus's teaching? He Himself was the teaching. He lived what He taught. He taught with authority. He prefaced some of His teaching by saying, "Most assuredly, I say to you" (NKJV John 3:3). He did not have to bring in other authorities to substantiate His statements. He spoke with the authority of God. "And God said. . . ." Jesus used ordinary, everyday things in

His teaching. He talked about a mustard seed, about birds of the air, about lilies of the field, and about planting seed. He taught by using stories. He told about a prodigal son who went away from home but returned when he had wasted everything and received a welcome from his waiting father. He told about a shepherd, who even though having 100 sheep, went out to search for one lost sheep. He told about a rich man who had everything but God, a poor man who had nothing but God, and the destinies they faced. He told about a wedding feast where many guests were invited, but they began to make excuses, so the man giving the feast invited the poor and needy to come instead.

Jesus taught us how to pray. The disciples asked Jesus to teach them how to pray. Jesus taught them by His own example, but He also gave them a model prayer. "Our Father in heaven, hallowed be Your name, Your kingdom come, Your will be done" (Matthew 6:9–10). On one occasion, Peter asked Jesus how many times he should forgive one who sinned against him. Peter thought seven times would surely be adequate. But Jesus said, not seven times, but seventy times seven. In other words, there is to be no limit to our forgiveness. We are not to use a calculator when it comes to forgiveness.

The Sermon on the Mount shows Jesus's surpassing ability as a teacher. He taught using the element of surprise as He gave the beatitudes. "Blessed are the poor in spirit, for theirs is the kingdom of heaven. Blessed are those who mourn, for they will be comforted" (Matthew 5:3–4). Never in a million years would those hearing Jesus have expected what He said. They would never think such people to be happy. Rather, they would expect just the opposite.

E. Stanley Jones said this about Jesus's teaching: "Many teachers of the world have tried to explain everything—they have explained little or nothing. Jesus explained little and changed everything. Jesus changes everything He touches. Call Him a man and you will have to change your ideas of what a man is[;] call Him God, and you will have to change your ideas of what God is. He is the one figure in history that is not local or national. He is the universal Christ. All nations feel at home with Him when they really know Him."[6]

From whatever perspective we look at Jesus, we see only perfection. He is a perfect man. He is a perfect teacher. He is the model, the mirror, and the goal for all mankind. He is the perfect Mediator between God and man because He is fully God and fully man. Here is One who fully understands our weaknesses because He became a man and lived here. Here is One who fully understands our sorrow and troubles because He saw them and bore our sorrows. These words assure us of this truth: "Jesus wept" (John 11:35).

CHAPTER 3

THERE'S NO ONE LIKE JESUS IN HIS MIRACLES

THERE HAVE BEEN MIRACLE WORKERS before Christ. God did miracles through many of the prophets. The apostles in the New Testament did miracles. And there have been other people in history who have claimed to do miracles. But never has there been a miracle worker like Jesus. He Himself is the great miracle. And when you believe in Him, the miracles are what you would expect Him to do.

Jesus never did miracles like a magician does, simply to get attention. Satan suggested that Jesus perform a miracle to satisfy His hunger by turning stones into bread. Jesus quoted from Scripture and refused. Satan further suggested that Jesus gain popularity and attention by jumping from the top of the temple. Again, Jesus rejected the temptation. He would not use His power in reckless or selfish ways. He had the power to call forth heaven's armies to deliver Him when soldiers came to arrest Him. He had the power to come down from the cross as people taunted Him, but He refused to use that power.

There was a restraint and selectivity in His miracles. He would not do miracles to satisfy the curiosity of Herod. Nor would He become a king, which many people wanted to meet their physical needs for bread. There was a purpose in all that He did. His miracles were acts of love to meet human need. They were revelations of His power over every conceivable situation. They were testimonies concerning His person. The miracles were called signs. They pointed to God. They declared the glory of Christ.

Colin Brown remarked, "They are tokens of a higher order that is ultimately more real than our world of change and decay."[7] He also said, "The signs and wonders belong to God's special saving acts, but they are not everyday occurrences."

Erich Sauer said this about miracles "A miracle is an expression of God's freedom; it does not result from the powers and presuppositions of natural life, but enters their context as something new from God."[8]

Jesus did many different miraculous things. He opened the eyes of the blind. He touched a leper so that his skin was restored as pure and fresh as a tiny baby's skin. He delivered wild demoniacs who were harming themselves and others. He raised Lazarus after he had been dead for four days by saying, "Lazarus, come out." Someone has commented that unless Jesus had used Lazarus's name, all the dead would have come out! When the disciples were afraid a storm would overturn their boat, Jesus stilled the storm, and they said, "What kind of man is this? Even the winds and the waves obey Him!" (Matthew 8:27b). When the crowd was weary from hunger, Jesus fed them by multiplying a small boy's fish and loaves. He lifted a crippled man and gave him a freedom he had never known. He spoke the word and a centurion's servant was healed, even though the servant was far away.

When we consider Jesus's life, we feel that miracles were natural for Him. It was not more difficult for Him to raise a dead man than it was to speak the worlds into existence. It was no more a problem for Him to heal the crippled and the lame than it was to create man in the beginning. All that He did fits in with who He was and what He came to do. As David Redding says, "All of Christ's miracles are spectacular, instantaneous, visible thrills, but the astounding wonder is the way they always go hand in hand with His good deeds, like a legible crown to His compassion."[9]

The transfiguration of Christ is not usually listed under His miracles, but it was certainly a supernatural event. And we will consider it briefly here, because it certainly shows the uniqueness of Jesus. Jesus took the three disciples closest to Him and went up a mountain. A cloud enshrouded them, and Jesus's countenance changed. His clothes began to shine. One of the Gospel writers says that His clothes were shining brighter than the sun. Another writer says that they were whiter than any fuller (cleaner) on earth could bleach them.

It is sometimes debated whether the light shining from Jesus was coming from within or without His body. Many people believe it was light coming from within. But it is possible that it was also light coming from above. The glory of Christ was shining through His earthly body. No doubt Peter was speaking about this when he wrote, "For He received honor and glory from God the Father when the voice came to Him from the Majestic Glory, saying, 'This is my Son, whom I love; with Him I am well pleased' (2 Peter 1:17). The disciples did not know what to say at the time. But they remembered forever this unusual manifestation of Jesus's glory.

Jesus told His disciples that He would die and be raised on the third day. And Jesus's resurrection from the dead is a miracle indeed. William Hendricks said, "The resurrection of Christ is the highest act in the historical drama of God. It is to be placed on a par with God's original act of creating the world and God's final act of changing the world."[10] It is clear that Jesus died on the cross. And the evidence is overwhelming that Jesus rose from the dead. He appeared several times to skeptical disciples. They believed only after they had seen Him. This victory over death fits perfectly with the miracle of His incarnation, the miracle of His perfect life, and all that Jesus taught. As He said, "I am the resurrection and the life" (John 11:25).

Here is what C. S. Lewis said about the miracles of Christ: "All the essentials of Hinduism would, I think, remain unimpaired if you subtracted the miraculous, and the same is almost true of

Mohammedanism. But you cannot do that with Christianity. It is precisely the story of a great Miracle. A naturalistic Christianity leaves out all that is specifically Christian."[11]

Phillip Schaff aptly said, "[Jesus] is the central miracle of the whole gospel history. All His miracles are but the natural manifestation of His miraculous person, and hence they were performed with the same ease with which we perform our ordinary daily works."[12] He further remarks, "It would be the greatest miracle indeed, if He, who is a miracle Himself, should have performed no miracles."

The miracles point to Jesus, who can meet the needs of all mankind. However small or great the need may be, however impossible or helpless the situation may be, He, the greatest Miracle of all, is able completely to supply the needs for every human situation.

The miracles of Jesus are foretastes of the future. He will come again in power and glory and raise the dead. The assurance of that is His own resurrection. There will even be a resurrection for the creation as all things are made new. Our souls and bodies will be transformed like unto His glorious body. It will be amazing indeed when there is no more crying, no more death, no more sickness, but only everlasting life, life with the Lord of Life.

We cannot dissect the miracles of Christ, nor can we put them under a microscope. We cannot explain them apart from Jesus who did them. There is always a mystery about His person and what He did. The miracles were unique. They cause us to fall in adoration before Jesus who was dead but is now alive.

CHAPTER 4

THERE'S NO ONE LIKE
JESUS IN HIS CREATION

WE SOMETIMES SAY THAT MAN created something. However, we never really create anything. We take things already in existence and change them. Jesus Christ spoke the worlds into existence before there was anything. That is the meaning of the word used in the first verse of the Bible: "In the beginning God created the heavens and the earth" (Genesis 1:1). There was no pre-existing material from which God created the universe.

In the Gospel of John, we learn that the creation came about through the power of Christ. "Through Him all things were made; without Him nothing was made that has been made" (John 1:3). This truth is stated again in Colossians 1:16–17: "For by Him all things were created: things in heaven and on earth, visible and invisible, whether thrones or powers or rulers or authorities; all things were created by Him and for Him. He is before all things, and in Him all things hold together." There can be no doubt about what is being said in these verses. Jesus Christ is the Creator of all things seen and unseen.

Creation did not just happen. In the same way, a beautiful picture does not just happen. There is an artist behind it. A stately building does not just happen. There is an architect behind it. An inspiring piece of music does not just happen. There is a musician behind it. An outstanding novel does not come to be by accident. There is a writer who planned it and wrote it. This amazing universe has a Creator. And there is no one like Him. He is Jesus Christ.

Consider some of the things that Christ has made. One night, I looked up into an African night sky, far away from the lights of modern cities, and the sky was blanketed with a carpet of light. It seemed that you could almost reach out and touch the stars. Astronomers tell us that there are billions and billions of stars in billions and billions of galaxies. The photos from NASA show beautiful patterns and designs in the constellations.

Once, I saw some of the giant sequoia trees. They soared into the heavens. It was a breathtaking experience. I was deeply moved. I found myself thinking, "How Great Thou Art." And the One responsible for those great trees is the One who once hung on a tree for us.

There is an almost endless variety of plants and flowers. Who made the fragrance of the orchids? Who made the delicate petals of the lily? Who made the tiny flowers that grace the mountainside? Who made the roses, which bring such delight on Valentine Day? There is only one answer, and that is the matchless Jesus.

The birds of the air and the different animals also point to an amazing artist and designer. Who has not marveled at the tiny hummingbird and its ability to hover like a helicopter? Who has not marveled at the majestic eagle coasting effortlessly through the sky? Who has not been surprised at the agility of a squirrel or the speed of a horse?

There is also the water world, in which there are countless varieties of fish and animals. Who would have thought of how a penguin cares for his young and how he survives? Who would have engineered a seal who can live in the water and also on the land? Who would have dreamed up the idea of a giant whale?

When we move to the infinitesimally small cells, we see the same beauty and design. There is a surprising complexity to the cell, and yet our body is made up of millions of cells. Each of them is a complex city in itself. If we consider the atom, there is also surprise and mystery. Richard A. Swenson said, "To count the atoms in a drop of water would require every human on earth counting one atom per second for twenty thousand years."[13] That's amazing!

The organs of the body are astounding creations. Thomas Dubay quotes from a United Airlines *Mainliner* magazine, "The brain weighs less than three pounds, but a computer capable of handling a single brain's output would cover the entire earth."[14]

What artist can adequately capture the awesome beauty of a sunrise or a sunset? What artist can do justice in painting the Himalaya Mountains? What artist can depict the beauty when all nature seems to come alive in the springtime with bursts of color everywhere?

How beautiful must be the Creator who made all this vast universe, the earth, and all the creatures who live here! The One who created this beauty must be indescribably beautiful in Himself! This beautiful Creator is beyond compare when it comes to the creation.

We must be careful to distinguish between the creation and the Creator. We do not worship the creation, even though it is magnificent. That would be idolatry. To worship the things He has made would be like a person who views a painting and talks to the painting, ignoring the artist nearby. It would be like talking to a manuscript of music and ignoring the musician beside you. This would be unthinkable. And yet there are people who will worship the things that Christ created and completely ignore His presence and person.

Not only did Christ create all things, but He also holds them all together. Why does this earth follow a predictable course year after year? Why do the planets move in precise motion? Why do objects thrown into the air come down again? It is all because Jesus holds it all together. Men may defy Christ, but He gives the very breath that we breathe. Even those who reject Him openly depend upon Him for their very physical life each moment of the day. It is in Him that all things hold together.

Have you ever wondered why there is a universe and why there is the Earth and life here? Paul gives the answer. It was all created for Him. "All things were created by Him and for Him." We know that He did not create us because of a need in Himself or in the Godhead. He created because He wanted to. He created to show His glory. He created out of the love of His heart.

The creation about us should cause us to sing as the African Christians do: "There's no one, there's no one like Jesus." He is the Creator. He is utterly unique, matchless, indescribable as the Creator. We were made for Him. And until we take our place as His created beings, we will always be out of place. Our place is face-down at the feet of Jesus!

CHAPTER 5

THERE'S NO ONE LIKE JESUS IN HIS REVELATION

THROUGH THE AGES PEOPLE HAVE sought to find out what God is like. Often the ideas of men were surprisingly like themselves. Many times their gods were bad characters who acted solely for themselves. Frequently, men's ideas about a god are little more than good luck charms. Many people would like to have a god they can carry around with them or put into a box. In other words, they would like to have a god whom they can control, a god who is subject to their will.

Jesus is the final revelation of God to men. In the Gospel of John, He is called "the Word." A word communicates. Jesus is God's final word to man. In the past God spoke to man in various ways. He spoke through the prophets. "But in these last days He has spoken to us by His Son, whom He appointed heir of all things, and through whom He made the universe. The Son is the radiance of God's glory and the exact representation of His being" (Hebrews

1:2–3a). Jesus has revealed perfectly what the Father wants us to know about Himself and His purpose for us. Jesus is the "exact representation of His being."

When people want to present supposed revelation from whatever source, we must reject it immediately. We cannot go beyond Jesus. And we will never go beyond Him. Jesus revealed the Father to us. He spoke of the Father as Abba. *Abba* is a term of affection used even today by Jewish children for their fathers. It means "daddy" or "papa." It is true that God is transcendent and far beyond what our feeble minds can conceive. But in Christ we are His children, and He wants us to feel close to Him. He is our Heavenly Daddy. And we can run to Him as a small child runs to his father when he is hurt and wants to be loved. Weak though we are, we can climb into the arms of our Heavenly Abba, because He delights in us.

Jesus brought God near to us. There is a great distance between who God is and who we are, but Jesus has bridged the gap. He brings us near to God. And although our understanding is limited now and will always be limited by our finiteness, we can understand the things that Jesus revealed about God. Philip, one of Jesus's disciples, asked how he could know the Father. This was Jesus's reply: "Anyone who has seen Me has seen the Father" (John 14:9b).

What are some of the things that Jesus revealed about God? He certainly revealed the love of God. We see this in the way that

He treated people. He was kind and good to despised and rejected people. He reached out to outcasts and to people that polite society ignored. He treated the lepers with dignity and compassion. He was never too tired to reach out to people in need. But the place where we see His love most clearly is on the cross, where He died for our sins. Early in his first epistle, John declared that "God is love." Later on, he tells us what love is and where we can see it. "This is love: not that we loved God, but that He loved us and sent His Son as an atoning sacrifice for our sins" (1 John 4:10). And the most well-known verse in all the Bible says, "For God so loved the world that He gave His one and only Son" (John 3:16a).

Jesus revealed the holiness of God. There was an "otherness" about Jesus. In His presence sinful men like Peter saw such a difference between His life and their own sinful lives that it was frightening. The Bible teaches that God is holy. He is just and righteous. And that is what we find Jesus revealing in His life and in His teaching. He drove the moneychangers out of the temple. When He wrote on the ground, the accusers of an immoral woman left one by one, convicted of their sin. Again, we see the holiness of God most clearly in the death of Jesus. Jesus paid the penalty for our sins. God never winks at sin or says that it doesn't matter.

In Jesus, we see how God is good. He is not just good part of the time, but He is always good. What is goodness? Look at Jesus and you will see it. He taught that God sends the rain on the just and on the unjust. He taught that it is not the healthy people who need a doctor but those who are sick.

The Bible says that "God is light" (1 John 1:5). And that is what Jesus revealed. He said, "I am the light of the world" (John 8:12). In Him we see God. There was not "a spark of divinity" in Him, such as people sometimes speak of. He was fully God! And He revealed God to us.

Our knowledge of God is limited by our frailties and natural inabilities. But I believe that we will ever be learning more about our Heavenly Father. We will ever be learning as we walk with Jesus and the Holy Spirit teaches us. God is so great that we will never come to the end of our learning, even after countless ages of time. An eternity will not be enough to understand fully the love, the holiness, the goodness, the righteousness, and all the greatness of the triune God.

Someone has spoken of Jesus as "God with skin on." When we look at Him, we are looking at God. Jesus is the perfect mirror showing the attributes of God. A mirror does not lie. It shows the image of the person standing before it. When we stand before Jesus by reading the New Testament, we see the perfect image of God.

The main characteristic of cults is that they always add something on to the revelation that God has given. It is often a new book in addition to the Bible. It is sometimes a person who claims to speak with the authority and in the place of Christ. In confronting false teaching, we need to remember these words of Jesus: "I am the Alpha and the Omega, the First and the Last, the

Beginning and the End" (Revelation 22:13). Peter once asked, "Lord, to whom shall we go? You have the words of eternal life. We believe and know that you are the Holy One of God" (John 6:68–69).

There is no one like Jesus, who reveals the heart of God and God's purpose for man. All we need, we find in Jesus. He is the end of our searching. He is the destination for all our questions about God. There will never be anyone like Jesus who has revealed God like He has. Our journey stops with Him. He brings us to the Father.

CHAPTER 6

THERE'S NO ONE LIKE JESUS IN HIS SALVATION

THERE HAS NEVER BEEN A rescue mission such as the one that Jesus undertook. When a tragedy happens, all the resources of a country are directed to rescuing people in danger. It is done carefully and quickly. Sometimes millions of dollars are spent in the rescue operation. It may go on for a long time, until all hope of rescue is over.

Jesus came to rescue us from sin. The rescue operation of Jesus was costly. It was the most costly rescue of all time. The cost was His own blood. We are reminded that the cost was not paid in silver or gold. There is no way that we can calculate such a cost. The cost is far beyond what we could pay together as sinful human beings. It was an infinite cost.

What is amazing about this salvation is that God planned it before the foundation of the world. Before the creation of man and before the existence of the earth, God planned to save us through the death of His Son. In Revelation 13:8 are these words: "The Lamb that was slain from the creation of the world." Before Adam and Eve rebelled, God had already made plans for their salvation. His plan was that we would be saved through the death of His Son Jesus.

Throughout the Old Testament, rivers of blood flowed as animals were slain and offered. Those sacrifices could never take away sin, but they did point to the coming of the perfect Lamb. They taught that man could not rescue himself. Unless there were a rescue from another source, there would be no rescue for us. We could not save ourselves. Only a perfect Lamb was acceptable. Only one Lamb could meet the necessary qualification. That Lamb was Jesus.

Jesus came for this one purpose: to give His life for us, to become our substitute for sin, to open the way into heaven. Jesus Himself is our salvation. When we have Jesus, we have complete salvation. Jesus did all that He came to do. On the cross He cried out, "It is finished." That means that Jesus completed the way of salvation. He completed what men had tried to do through their own efforts. Jesus paid for all our sin. His blood atoned for our sins. There at the cross all of our sins—past, present, and future—were laid on Jesus. It was as if Jesus became sin for us. "God made Him who had no sin to be sin for us, so that in Him we might become the righteousness of God" (2 Corinthians 5:21).

Jesus took our sin and by faith we receive His righteousness. We are justified by faith. We are covered by the righteousness of Jesus. When God looks at us, He sees the perfect righteousness of Jesus. Jesus took away our guilt and condemnation. Through His death we are reconciled to God. His blood has made peace possible with God. The war is over. We are also adopted into the family of God through what Jesus did. Not only that, but we are also sanctified in position before a holy God. Everything that we need, everything that we could possibly need, we have in Christ. It is not Christ "and" but Christ "only."

The uniqueness of this salvation is found in the words "in Christ." Those words are repeated many times in the epistles of Paul. They show the position and the relationship we have with Christ. It is a vital union with Christ. We remain who we are as persons, but Christ lives within us. And our spiritual address becomes "in Christ." God accepts us as He accepts Jesus. He loves us as He loves Jesus. Our very life depends upon Christ now and always. One pastor pointed out that we will need Christ in the future just as much as we need Him now.

This good news thrills us. Jesus has done it all. Salvation is complete. It is a gift. All we can do is to receive freely what Christ has done for us. This is made so clear in the book of Hebrews. There it speaks of Jesus being seated at the right hand of God. He is seated because the work of salvation is complete. Several times in the book of Hebrews we read the expression "once for all." Never will a sacrifice for sin have to be offered again. Never will there need to be another cross. One time only is sufficient for all eternity. The Old Testament sacrifices were offered continuously. They were offered week after week, year after year, because they were only types. In Jesus we have the final sacrifice. Jesus is no longer upon the cross and He will never be there again.

When Jesus returned to heaven, He did not take the sacrifices of animals. "He did not enter by means of the blood of goats and calves; but He entered the Most Holy Place once for all by His own blood, having obtained eternal redemption" (Hebrews 9:12). Today the Lamb of God is our only plea. Not who we are, not what we have done: only the blood of Jesus is sufficient for our salvation.

In our familiarity with it, we may forget how different and marvelous this good news is. All the religions of the world basically teach that man must save himself. Their message is "do it yourself." But the salvation found in Jesus is already done. Nothing less and nothing more than Jesus Himself is our salvation. We may be a new Christian, or we may be a follower of Christ for many years. We may be a small boy or girl, or we may be a gray-headed man or woman. We may be a robust youth, or we may be lying on our deathbed. Whatever our state, there is only one hope for all of us. It is the blood of the Lamb slain from the foundation of the world.

Our message must always be proclaimed: "Come to Jesus." He is the way, the truth, and the life. There is no other name by which we can be saved. Like Paul, "we preach Christ." There is no other one who died in our place and paid completely our sin debt. Therefore we say, "Look to Jesus and live." The Bible says that grace and truth came through Jesus Christ. Our salvation is all through the grace of Jesus. We do not deserve what He did or what He gives. We all must come in the same way. We all must come to the cross. Michael Horton wrote, "This gospel—the Good News of God's justification of sinners in Christ—is not a means to a greater end. It is not one theme among many. It is not something we use in order to go on to something more important, more relevant, and more practical. It is the ocean that we swim in, the air that we breathe, the identity that defines us."[15]

The old gospel song says it well:

What can wash away my sin? Nothing but the blood of Jesus;

What can make me whole again? Nothing but the blood of Jesus.

This is all my hope and peace, Nothing but the blood of Jesus;

This is all my righteousness, Nothing but the blood of Jesus.[16]

CHAPTER 7

THERE'S NO ONE LIKE JESUS IN HIS INTERCESSION

ONE OF THE MOST DESPERATE feelings we can have is to need help and to find no one available to help. It may be a situation where a person could not help even if we called them. At other times we may call someone, only to find that they could help but not at the time when we need them most. Job was surrounded by friends who came to comfort him, but none of them understood him. When they tried to help, they made matters worse. In his distress Job cries out, wishing for a mediator, someone who could stand between him and a holy God. What Job and many other people have sought is found in Jesus.

Jesus is a Mediator. "For there is one God and one mediator between God and men, the man Christ Jesus" (1 Timothy 2:5). Jesus is the bridge between God and man. He takes us by the hand and brings us to the Father. When Adam and Eve sinned, they were afraid and tried to hide from God. God took the initiative and came seeking for them. He asked, "Where are you?" When we have failed and are afraid, we have a Mediator who comes looking for us.

Not only is Jesus our Mediator, but He is also our Advocate. When Jesus spoke of His going away, the disciples were sad. Jesus assured them that He would not leave them as orphans but that He would send another Comforter. And that means another Comforter just like Him. The word comforter is translated variously as "helper", "advocate", or "counselor". It is a picture of someone who comes beside us for support. This idea is expressed well in these words: "My dear children, I write this to you so that you will not sin. But if anybody does sin, we have one who speaks to the Father in our defense—Jesus Christ, the Righteous One" (1 John 2:1). When Satan attacks us like he did to Job, there is One who stands in heaven on our behalf. No accusation will go beyond the Savior who is both God and man, our Advocate before the Father.

When people tell us that they are praying for us, we are encouraged. How much more should we be encouraged to know that Jesus is our Great High Priest. In the book of Hebrews, the writer teaches us the significance of this reality. Jesus can sympathize with us perfectly. He understands our burdens and our sorrows. Jesus experienced many of the same things we experience. He was tempted, rejected, hated, betrayed, and He experienced sorrow.

In our greatest times of need, above all, we need someone who understands and someone who will stand with us. During sorrow, it is a comfort when a friend comes who has gone through the same sorrow. When they say, "I understand; I know how you feel," it helps us bear our sorrow. When a friend who has experienced cancer shares about that experience with a cancer patient, she is encouraged. Jesus does understand whatever we may be going through. He knows how to pray as none of us could possibly know.

What is so different about Jesus? It is that He not only understands us but that He also intercedes for us. Jesus not only has the desire to help, but He also has the ability to do so. A promise to pray from a fellow Christian is wonderful. How about a promise from Jesus to pray for us! In Hebrews 7:25, it says that "He always lives to intercede for them." This High Priest is described in verse 26: "Such a high priest meets our need—one who is holy, blameless . . . above the heavens."

We see an illustration of Jesus's praying for believers in the case of Peter. Peter was proud and confident that he would never fail to follow Jesus. But Jesus knew that Peter would soon fail terribly. He assured Peter that He would pray for him. And Peter was later restored and became a powerful witness for Christ. Someone is always praying for us: Jesus, at the right hand of the Father. Not only is Jesus praying for us, but the Holy Spirit also makes intercession for us. These things encourage us to run to our Heavenly Father and not hide away in despair. "Let us then approach the throne of grace with confidence, so that we may receive mercy and find grace to help us in our time of need" (Hebrews 4:16).

One thing that sets Jesus apart from all other priests is that His priesthood is unchanging. It is eternal. In the Bible there is a strange figure mentioned, whose name is Melchizedek. Nothing is known about his beginning or his ending. He is a type of Christ, who has no beginning and no ending. In Old Testament times, the priests were in constant change. They would serve for a few years and then they would be replaced. They were marked by change. But there is no succession of high priests to follow Jesus. He is eternal. What He has always done, He continues to do. What the early Christians experienced in their lives, we experience today because He is the same Jesus who is our Intercessor.

The same person who is our Savior is also our Advocate, our Mediator, and our Intercessor. There is no one like Jesus. He does not put us on the journey to life and then leave us to fend for ourselves. Instead, He walks with us, stands beside us, and even represents us before our Heavenly Father. We are not numbers on a pegboard, but redeemed ones with a Redeemer, children of God with an Elder Brother, disciples with a Master. He knows our names. We belong to Him and He belongs to us. He is both the Author and the Finisher of our faith.

Jesus is a man of prayer. On earth Jesus often withdrew from the disciples and prayed. There is no doubt that He often prayed for His disciples. We find a good example of the way Jesus prayed in John 17. There He asked the Father to keep His followers. He also prayed that they would be with Him and see His glory. There is also the intense prayer shortly before His death. In the garden as He prayed, perspiration like drops of blood fell from His face. He prayed, "Not my will, but your will be done." Is this not the prayer that He prays for us? A man of prayer is the Lamb upon the throne. There is no one like Jesus!

CHAPTER 8

THERE'S NO ONE LIKE JESUS IN HIS CHURCH

THERE ARE MANY DIFFERENT KINDS of organizations: political, social, educational, economic, and religious. Often the members are grouped together because of the same ethnic characteristics, economic status, or political philosophy. The church is different than any other organization. It would really be better to call it an organism, rather than an organization. It is alive and receives its life from the Head of the church, Jesus Christ. Without Christ, there is no church, just as there is no living body without the head. The church draws its life from the Head of the church.

We see the unique relationship of Jesus to the churches in the book of Revelation. There John sees the living Christ standing among the churches. He is not a disinterested spectator withdrawn from the action. He is engaged fully and related to each of the churches, despite their differences and weaknesses. Many of those churches were struggling as they faced persecution and corruption from within. Jesus speaks words to each of the churches. To the church at Smyrna, He says, "These are the words of Him who is the First and the Last, who died and came to life again" (Revelation 2:8b).

Several figures of speech are used to explain the relationship between Christ and the church. The church is compared to a temple where Christ is the Chief Cornerstone. It is compared to a bride, and Christ is the Bridegroom. We are called a "royal priesthood," but Christ is the Great High Priest. All these comparisons show that the church is dependent completely upon Jesus Christ.

The word *church* is used in two ways in the New Testament. Most often, it refers to a local assembly of believers. Sometimes it is used in a universal sense to include all believers in Christ. In the universal sense, all believers are one in Christ. Divisions in society, divisions among nations, divisions according to wealth, all vanish away. And the same should be true in local churches. "There is neither Jew nor Greek, slave nor free, male nor female, for you are all one in Christ Jesus" (Galatians 3:28).

Jesus not only established the church, but He also guaranteed its victory. Along the way, the church suffers what some would call extinction or destruction. But it always rises from the ashes. It is sometimes knocked down. In God's timing and through His power, it marches through battle losses toward final victory. Jesus said this about His church: "On this rock I will build my church, and the gates of Hades will not overcome it" (Matthew 16:18b). No one else could guarantee the success of any organization before it had even begun. And who would predict success with a small band of fishermen as leaders? But that is what happened. The resurrection of Christ transformed these men. And a mighty movement of God began when Jesus sent the Holy Spirit, the Comforter.

The mission of the church can only be accomplished through the presence and power of the Founder, Jesus Christ. There is no other Founder like Jesus. Other organizations continue without the founder. There would be no church and could be no church without the ever-living Founder, Jesus. Our mission is all related to Him. We preach Christ. We teach Christ. He is the center of the church. He is the message of the church.

Churches meet in the name of Christ. We meet together to worship the blessed Trinity: Father, Son, and Holy Spirit. Christ is at the heart of our worship. We sing about Him. We pray in His name. And this is the confidence we have as we meet together: if only two or three believers are meeting in His name, He is present. The presence of Christ is essential for our very existence.

I have visited churches in many different countries. Sometimes they meet in houses. They may meet in an unfinished building. The shade of a tree may be the meeting place. Occasionally, they meet on the upper floor of a business building. Their indigenous music is different. Their styles of worship vary. But something is always the same: the presence of Christ and His relationship to His people. There is a oneness and unity despite the differences.

The Christian feels at home even with these differences. The song says it well: "In Christ there is no East or West, in Him no North or South, but one great fellowship of love throughout the whole wide earth."[17]

The mission of the church is to take the gospel of Christ to all people. Always Christ is to be the power and the heart of our message. It is the fospel of Christ. It is all about Him. And without Him the church has no message. Without Him it has no reason for existence. Jesus is everything in the church and everything for the church. The church is in Him. The church moves forward with Him. The church follows after Him. The church triumphs through Him.

It is not enough to call a group of people a church just because they meet together. The distinguishing mark of the church is this: it belongs to Christ. It proclaims Christ and what He has done. It worships Christ. And while churches today are often soiled and fall short of Christ's plans for them, we can be sure that Christ stands among the churches. He is working out His purposes in the churches. And one day the church will be presented to the Bridegroom in spotless robes. There is no one like Jesus when it comes to the church!

CHAPTER 9

THERE'S NO ONE LIKE JESUS IN HIS NAMES

TO SPEAK ABOUT THE NAMES of Jesus is like stepping into a lovely garden. Each flower has a beauty of its own. There are the roses, lilies, irises, dahlias, and snapdragons. There are smaller flowers like the flowering moss, petunias, and geraniums. There are peonies, azaleas, and flowering trees. And there are unique fragrances. Jesus has so many names, because each name tells us something about Him. He is so wonderful that many names must be used to describe Him and express His character.

Charles J. Rolls wrote five books concerning the names and titles of Jesus. Here we will discuss only a few of His many names. Probably the most familiar name is the name *Jesus*. In the Old Testament we find a similar name, *Joshua*. *Smith's Bible Dictionary* says that it is the Hebrew name that is the origin of the name Jesus. An angel told Joseph that Jesus was to be His name because

He would save people from their sins. This name, then, especially speaks of Jesus as our Savior.

Bruce Marchiano asks, "How does one describe One who is utterly indescribable? Is there a word that means joy but is beyond incomprehensible joy? A word that encompasses the thunder of every waterfall, the dance of every brook, the laughter of every baby in the nestle of every daddy's arms?"[18] He answers, "It is the word of words. The single word that every human life right along with its every human hope and struggle is answered by and resolved in. It is the beginning and it is the end. It is the fullness of life, the gateway to eternity, the hope of the ages. It is . . . Jesus."

Prince of Peace is another name that belongs uniquely to Jesus. This name is found in the book of Isaiah. Jesus came to bring peace to men. It was the message that the heavenly host brought to the shepherds at the time of His birth. It is the legacy that Jesus left us. Shortly before His death, He spoke about His peace and said that He would give us peace. It is what happened at the cross. Jesus made a way of peace, a way of reconciliation for us. "For He Himself is our peace, who has made the two one and has destroyed the barrier, the dividing wall of hostility" (Ephesians 2:14). Only One has broken down the barriers between a holy God and sinful man.

The favorite name that Jesus used for Himself is *Son of Man*. The *Evangelical Dictionary of Theology* points out that this name is used 69 times in the Synoptic Gospels and 13 times in the Gospel of John.[19] It is a name that especially points to Jesus as the Messiah. He is the anointed one, the promised one. I believe that it also points to Jesus's identification with man. In the book of Romans, He is called "the second Adam." In His baptism at the hands of John the Baptist, He was identifying with man. And in using this name, Jesus fulfills all the promises made about His coming and points to His mission in coming as the Messiah. Notice how Jesus used this name concerning Himself: "For the Son of Man came to seek and to save what was lost" (Luke 19:10).

Jesus is called the *Lion of the tribe of Judah*. Many of the kings came from Judah. David was one of those kings. And Jesus came in that lineage. He fulfilled the promise made to David concerning the throne. A lion is known for its strength and its majesty. It is considered the king of beasts. C. S. Lewis used the lion as a symbol for Christ in his children's stories. Used together with this title for Christ is another that might strike you as very strange— the Lamb of God. Jesus is both. He is the Lamb of God at the same time that He is the Lion of the tribe of Judah. He is tender as a Lamb but strong like a Lion. He is the sacrifice for our sins, but He is also Lord of all, King Jesus.

We do not hear this name as much as many of the others. But it is a wonderful name: the *Lord of glory*. One translation says "glorious Lord." Jesus manifested His glory while He lived here on earth. "The Word became flesh and made His dwelling among us. We have seen His glory, the glory of the One and Only, who came from the Father, full of grace and truth" (John 1:14). Some Bible teachers point out that glory includes all the attributes of God together. Moses wanted to see God's glory. The Lord hid Moses because he could not see all of God's glory and live. When the Lord passed by, Moses saw only the back parts of God. In the book of Revelation, John fell like a dead man when he saw the Lord of glory after His resurrection.

There is a unique glory that belongs to God alone. Jesus gave the disciples a brief glimpse of that glory when He was transfigured on the mountain. Jesus is glorious, and one day the veil will be removed and we will see the King in His beauty. *Lord of glory* expresses clearly who Jesus is. He is God in the flesh. This is how Steve DeWitt described *glory*: "Glory to us looks like light. It is bright. It is radiant. But it is not light. It is like light, only whiter and purer. If we could capture a beam of glory light and put it under a microscope, we would discover that it is much different than a sunbeam. A sunbeam carries within it the nature of the sun. Glory light carries the likeness of God Himself. It is a visible expression of the nature of God."[20]

Some names are not found in the Bible directly, but because of what Jesus did, we may use them properly. One such name is *Redeemer*. Long ago, Job had expressed his faith by saying that he knew that his Redeemer lives. The New Testament speaks clearly about Christ redeeming us. Christ is our redemption. "In Him we have redemption through His blood, the forgiveness of sins, in accordance with the riches of God's grace" (Ephesians 1:7). This word depicts someone who goes into a slave market and buys slaves and then gives them freedom. Jesus opened the prison doors through His substitutionary death on the cross.

Another name that we can use appropriately for Jesus is the *Heavenly Bridegroom.* The church is called the bride of Christ. The book of Revelation speaks of the marriage supper of the Lamb. This Bridegroom loves His bride and waits expectantly for her. Our Heavenly Bridegroom gave Himself for the church. And the church is being made ready to meet the Bridegroom. This is amazing love, that He wants us to be with Him, that He wants us to experience His glory, that He wants us to live with Him forever. "As a bridegroom rejoices over his bride, so will your God rejoice over you" (Isaiah 62:5b).

No other person has names like Jesus. His names stand for His person. And no one else can do what is meant by those names. All these beauties, all these fragrances, and all these praises belong to One alone, the Lord Jesus Christ. As Charles H. Spurgeon said, "Jesus is a song in one word. Jesus is a matchless oratorio in two syllables. Jesus is all the hallelujahs of eternity in five letters."[21] John Newton, better known for the hymn "Amazing Grace," also wrote the hymn "How Sweet the Name of Jesus Sounds."

How sweet the name of Jesus sounds

In a believer's ear!

It soothes his sorrows, heals his wounds,

And drives away his fear,

And drives away his fear.[22]

CHAPTER 10

THERE'S NO ONE LIKE JESUS IN HIS FRIENDSHIP

GREAT FRIENDSHIPS ARE OFTEN THE basis for novels and movies. The Bible tells us about some amazing friendships. Probably the most well-known is the friendship between David and Jonathan. They were committed to stand beside each other in life or death. They sealed their friendship with a blood covenant. Even after Jonathan's death, David looked after Jonathan's crippled son, Mephibosheth. Usually a new king would destroy people whom he thought would be a threat to his rule, but David brought Jonathan's son into the royal household.

Even the greatest friendships pale in comparison to Jesus and His friendship. Usually, our friendships are rather exclusive. We choose people like ourselves, or people who can help us. Jesus was a friend to many different kinds of people. Some of them were the outcasts of society. Some of them would even be considered enemies. Even among His closest friends there was a tremendous difference.

Jesus was called "a friend of tax collectors and 'sinners'" (Matthew 11:19). It was meant to be derogatory, but it was also true. Jesus went to the homes of people whom polite society scorned. One day, He went home with Zacchaeus. In Jewish society at that time, one of the most hated people was a tax collector. They were notorious for their dishonesty. They were considered traitors because they worked for the Roman government and collected taxes from their fellow Jews. They pocketed much of the money, which they collected for themselves. This enabled them to live a comfortable lifestyle, but it also isolated them. Usually, it meant they had few friends. Jesus visited with Zacchaeus and was kind to him. He talked to him as he would to "respectable" people. It is no surprise that Zacchaeus turned from his old way of life and became a believer in Christ.

One of Jesus's disciples was a former tax collector. He had lived a life of rejection for many years. But when he met Jesus, he heard Jesus's invitation, "Follow me." Who would have chosen such a man to write the Gospel of Matthew? But that is what this friend of Jesus did. Jesus saw in His friends not only where they were but also where they would go through His friendship.

Among the twelve disciples was Judas. For three years Jesus showed love and patience toward Judas. Jesus knew what Judas would do. We would have called Judas an enemy, because Judas was in the group for himself. He was taking money from the treasury. Who would want to be a friend with someone who would plot your murder? But Jesus spent many hours with Judas. Judas heard the teachings of Jesus and saw His miracles. But there was always something more interesting for Judas. He took advantage of the opportunities he had, but only to betray the one who said, "Love your enemies."

Obviously, certain friends were closer to Jesus than others. Jesus would sometimes take Peter, James, and John for something special. They went with Him to the Mount of Transfiguration. There were times when He went to the home of Mary, Martha, and their brother, Lazarus. Jesus spoke of Lazarus as "our friend." Friends enjoy each other's company. But there was an added dimension to Jesus's friendship. He loved with the deepest kind of love, the love that wants the best for the other person. When Jesus came to raise Lazarus from the dead and people saw the tears of Jesus, they said, "See how He loved him" (John 11:36b).

Friendship is often a rather fragile thing. Friends leave over disagreements. The fellowship and relationship are broken permanently in many cases. There is no friend like Jesus when it comes to enduring friendship. He does not give up on us. Time after time, the disciples would not understand, or they would do stupid things. But Jesus stayed with them. He explained things to them. Sometimes He would explain something many times. Jesus did all He told them He would do. His love was unchangeable. It was not dependent upon the faithfulness of His followers.

Peter even denied Jesus after he had boasted that he would never forsake him. He did the very thing that he thought he could not do. At the time of the crucifixion of Jesus, all the other disciples forsook Jesus also. At the hour when He needed them most, they left in fear. In the Garden of Gethsemane, the disciples all went to sleep while Jesus agonized in prayer. When they traveled toward Samaria one day and faced prejudice directly, they asked Jesus if they should call down fire from heaven to destroy the Samaritans. So many times they did not understand and did ill-advised things. The one constant in it all was the faithful friendship of Jesus. He did not abandon Peter, but restored him.

Unlike many friends, Jesus is always available. In a crisis we need a friend who will be with us, a friend who understands us, a friend who will help us. And that is what Jesus is. Erich Sauer commented that "Jesus never disappoints: Jesus only wonderfully surprises."[23] If we are looking for an enduring friendship, we will find it in Jesus. He said that He would not call us servants but friends. There is this insightful statement in Proverbs that Jesus completely fulfills. "There is a friend who sticks closer than a brother" (Proverbs 18:24b).

G. Campbell Morgan said, "My Friend never forgets me, never deserts me. He does not find any in high heaven in whom He takes a greater interest than He takes in me." "My Friend is so gentle. He might crush me even by the inflow of His strength. He might blind me by the very vision of His glory, but He does not.

He bends over me and says, 'I have many things to say unto you, but ye cannot bear them now.'"[24]

There was an intensity about the friendships of Jesus. He really cared about others. This intensity is seen in His words and His actions. All people mattered to Him. The boundaries of His friendship were wide enough to include anyone, even His enemies. Jesus taught us to love our enemies, and He practiced what He taught. He was a friend to the poor, the outcast, and the helpless.

J. Wilbur Chapman penned the words of a lovely hymn that goes like this:

Jesus! What a friend for sinners!

Jesus! Lover of my soul;

Friends may fail me,

Foes assail me,

He, my Savior, makes me whole.

Hallelujah! What a Savior!

Hallelujah! What a friend!

Saving, helping, keeping, loving,

He is with me to the end.[25]

CHAPTER 11

THERE'S NO ONE LIKE JESUS IN HIS EVANGELISM

EVANGELISTS COME AND GO. SOME are more effective than others. Sometimes they use questionable methods. Their lives may not be what you would expect from an evangelist. Their evangelism may be piecemeal. They may evangelize during professional times but do little at other times. This is where Jesus is unique. Evangelism was a lifestyle for Jesus. It was as natural as breathing air. He began His public ministry by telling people to repent because the kingdom of God was near.

It was not drudgery for Jesus to do evangelism. He said this about His mission: "'My food', said Jesus, 'is to do the will of Him who sent me and to finish His work'" (John 4:34). It was Jesus's joy to meet the spiritual needs of people. Nothing deterred Jesus. He made a straight line to the cross. He came to die for us. It was His mission to save us. Always there was the shadow of a cross as He traveled and spoke. He knew what was before Him. He was on a rescue mission. What was God's will for Jesus? It was what Jesus did while He was here. Jesus called it His food.

Another thing that distinguishes Jesus in evangelism is the urgency with which He did it. There was no procrastination. Jesus proclaimed the message wherever He went. It did not matter whether He was tired or not. It did not matter whether people were rich or poor. It did not matter whether they were outcasts or part of the social elite. There was no prejudice in Jesus.

Jesus went to people. Often in evangelism today, Christians call for people to come to a church. This is all right, but if we are to reach the masses of people, we must follow Jesus's method, which was to go to the people. It is not that Jesus neglected the crowds. He went to the crowds as well as individuals. We will be far more effective when we go to people with the message of Jesus.

In His evangelism, Jesus did something that we cannot do: He asked people to come and follow Him. We do not ask people to follow us. Our message is for people to come to Christ. Jesus said, "Come to me." We say, "Come to Jesus." Jesus said, "Follow me." We say, "Follow Jesus." Only Jesus can save. Our job is to point people to Jesus. We are to take people by the hand and bring them to Jesus.

One of the greatest failures in evangelism is the failure to mentor people in evangelism. The disciples of Jesus saw Jesus in action. They watched how He talked to people. They learned His methods. Jesus sent them out with the message. These were not highly educated people, but other people noticed that they had been with Jesus. Jesus was their message. They talked about His death and resurrection. The Holy Spirit empowered them and guided their words. As a result, multitudes came to Christ. We can multiply ourselves by mentoring others in evangelism. Andrew brought his brother Peter to Jesus. Andrew's life was then multiplied many times when Peter won many people to Christ.

What made Jesus so effective in evangelism? Jesus related to people at the point of their need. To the Samaritan woman at the well, Jesus talked about the living water, water that could quench the spiritual thirst in her soul. That living water was Jesus. In His dying moments on a cross, one of the thieves cried out, asking Jesus to remember him. Jesus said, "Today you will be with Me in paradise" (Luke 23:43b). To a woman accused of immorality, Jesus asked if anyone condemned her. Jesus said that He did not condemn her either and then told her to go and sin no more.

Jesus did not lower the bar in order to gain more followers. Many people were with Him when He gave them bread, but when He talked about His death for them, many of His listeners turned away. Jesus talked to a rich young ruler. This young man was interested, but when Jesus told him what he needed to do, he was unwilling to turn away from his materialistic lifestyle. Sadly, he went away.

Jesus used no high-pressure techniques. He warned people. He talked about hell. He pointed clearly to specific needs in people. Never did He beat people over their heads and force them into a decision. He did not want the love of a robot. He did not want unwilling followers. There is no example of Jesus buttonholing people and dragging them by the hair of their heads into His kingdom.

Compassion marked Jesus's evangelism. When He saw the crowds of people and saw them scattered and in need, He was moved with compassion. It was the same with individuals whom Jesus met. They knew that He cared, even if they turned away. Whether it was a leper, a religious leader, or a tax collector, Jesus had compassion. Compassion is love in action. It is love that feels the needs of others.

Jesus's vision for evangelism dwarfs the thoughts of men. Jesus thought not just about the people around Him; He had a world vision. This vision is expressed in the Great Commission: "Therefore go and make disciples of all nations, baptizing them in the name of the Father and of the Son and of the Holy Spirit, and teaching them to obey everything I have commanded you" (Matthew 28:19–20a). Wherever evangelists go today, Jesus is the message we take. We are assured of having His presence as we go.

The work of evangelism continues. The message is the same: Jesus. The methods change with modern technology. The one constant is Jesus. Jesus is ever the object and the power for evangelism. There's no one like Jesus in the work of evangelism.

CHAPTER 12

THERE'S NO ONE LIKE JESUS IN HIS SERVICE

THROUGHOUT HUMAN HISTORY THERE HAVE been many people who were admirable examples of service to others. Often they are unknown and unnoticed. They quietly go about doing good. In the church I attend, there are people like that. They are the quiet heroes of the faith who simply do what needs to be done without being asked.

Mother Teresa is one such person. She served people who were left to die on the streets of Calcutta, India. Serving others was a life ministry for her. We admire her selflessness as she ministered to the poorest of the poor.

Jesus is the unsurpassed example of service. He is unsurpassed in what He said about service and what He did in service. One day, the mother of two of the disciples came with them to make a special request. She asked that they might have places of honor in His kingdom. Jesus told them that they did not know what they were asking. Then He taught them about service. The common idea then was to get ahead of others, to elevate yourself into a position of authority. Jesus said, "Not so with you. Instead, whoever wants to become great among you must be your servant, and whoever wants to be first must be your slave—just as the Son of Man did not come to be served, but to serve, and to give His life as a ransom for many" (Matthew 20:26–28).

What Jesus said must have blown the minds of the disciples. It was revolutionary. That is exactly what Jesus demonstrated in His life. He showed that it is better to give than to receive. He revealed that joy is found in serving. It is not in asking, "What can I get out of this?" Joy comes when we ask, "What can I do in this situation to minister to others?" Jesus did not sit in an ivory tower and wait for people to minister to Him. On the contrary, He went to hurting people and gave Himself to serve them.

Jesus told about a good Samaritan. A man was seriously wounded, lying on the road. Most people passed by. They saw him but would not lift a finger to help. Maybe they reasoned that someone else would help. After all, they were busy. It was only the unexpected person who rendered aid. He came to the wounded man, provided for him, and even took care of his future needs when he had to leave. This parable was an expression of the way Jesus lived. He lived a life of generosity. He was generous with His time. He was generous with His abilities. He is the Great Physician. And wherever we find Jesus, He is ministering.

One of the most amazing examples of service is when Jesus washed the feet of His disciples. Washing feet was the job of a slave. It was one of the lowliest jobs anyone could do. It would be like the job of cleaning toilets in a public facility. Jesus showed that what is important is our attitude and motive in service, not the specific job. Our attitude should be the overriding factor in service. None of the disciples volunteered for this service. Maybe they waited for one of them to volunteer, but there was no one. Jesus took a towel and began to wash the feet of the disciples. John Ortberg has written, "He wore the garb of a slave, took the position of a slave, did the work of a slave, and suffered the death of a slave."[26]

Does ministry matter today? It does if we follow Jesus. Jesus said, "I have set you an example that you should do as I have done for you" (John 13:15). We all need examples when it comes to service. And Jesus is the supreme example. If we look for heroes, we will often be disappointed. As Christians, we are to look to Jesus. He is always our example when it comes to service. No one served like Jesus.

It took the disciples a long time before they finally understood Jesus's teaching concerning service. I believe they learned most of all from Jesus's example. Peter obviously did, because this is what he wrote: "To this you were called, because Christ suffered for you, leaving you an example, that you should follow in His steps" (1 Peter 2:21). Paul understood this, because he spoke of Christ becoming poor for us in order that we could become rich. Wherever you find followers of Christ, you will find people serving. Christ lives within us, and He continues to serve and minister through His followers.

Effective leaders are servants. Jesus was called a servant long before He came to the earth. And Jesus was a great Leader. He led as He served. Jesus spoke of Himself as the Good Shepherd. A shepherd leads sheep to quiet streams, to green pastures, and to resting places. The shepherd also protects the sheep. In other words, he serves the sheep. He cares for them. He stays with them and provides for their needs. That is what Jesus was always doing. He stayed with the sheep. To harm the sheep, an enemy would have to harm Him. The great need today is for servant leaders. And Jesus is the greatest Servant Leader. In His steps we will serve His people.

Jesus once talked about a time of judgment. He said that people would ask, "When did we see you naked or hungry or in prison?" Jesus said that when we provide clothes for needy people, we are doing it to Him. When we supply food for the hungry, we are doing it to Him. When we visit prisoners, we are doing it to Him. When we think of service in this way, it takes on a much greater dimension. Paul said that we are to do all things as unto the Lord. Even the most menial job will look different when we do it for Jesus.

We are most apt to find Jesus in lowly places. He will be in places of great suffering and need. Wherever people are ministering in

His name, we can be sure that Jesus is there. It has always been true. Jesus is the same today as when He washed the feet of His disciples. Mike Nappa describes Jesus's service perfectly: "One is not great because He serves; He serves because He is great."[27]

CHAPTER 13

THERE'S NO ONE LIKE JESUS IN HIS WISDOM

SOLOMON IS CONSIDERED TO BE one of the wisest men of all time. When the Lord asked Solomon at the beginning of his reign what he wanted, Solomon did not ask for riches or for a long life. Rather, he asked for wisdom that he might lead the people in the right way. The book of Proverbs speaks much about wisdom. Solomon is believed to have written many of these proverbs. He writes that wisdom is better than any precious metals or jewels. Wisdom is personified in these words: "I was there when he set the heavens in place, when he marked out the horizon on the face of the deep . . . Then I was the craftsman at his side. I was filled with delight day after day, rejoicing always in his presence" (Proverbs 8:27, 30). Some Bible scholars believe those words are talking about Christ.

People from different countries came to listen to Solomon's wisdom. The Queen of Sheba did not believe the reports she heard until she talked with Solomon herself. Then she knew that the reports had not been exaggerated: Solomon's wisdom was far greater than she had been told. "The whole world sought audience with Solomon to hear the wisdom God had put in his heart" (1 Kings 10:24). As great as Solomon's wisdom was, it pales before Wisdom Himself. "Now one greater than Solomon is here" (Matthew 12:42b).

Even before Jesus was born, Isaiah wrote, "The Spirit of the Lord will rest on Him—the Spirit of wisdom and of understanding, the Spirit of counsel and of power, the Spirit of knowledge and of the fear of the Lord" (Isaiah 11:2). As a child, the wisdom of God was manifested in Jesus's life. That is seen clearly when He goes to the temple as a twelve-year-old boy and talks with the religious leaders there. "And Jesus grew in wisdom and stature, and in favor with God and men" (Luke 2:52).

Some people have knowledge but they lack wisdom. Jesus had both knowledge and wisdom. Wisdom is the ability to use knowledge properly. It is the ability to discern things and make right choices. In wisdom, there is balance. In Jesus, nothing was out of line. His physical life, His spiritual life, His social life, and His emotional life all fit together perfectly. His emotions did not override His spiritual life. His physical needs did not overpower His social life. Wisdom is knowledge under control for God's purposes.

We see Jesus's wisdom in the way He treated His enemies. They were constantly after Him. They accused Him of breaking the Sabbath day. Jesus replied that they themselves even lifted an animal from a pit on the Sabbath. He pointed out that even David ate the consecrated bread on the Sabbath when he was traveling. They tried to trap Jesus by asking Him if they should pay taxes to Caesar. Jesus told them to pay taxes to whomever taxes were due.

On occasion Jesus countered their question with a question of His own. They asked Him what authority He had to do what He was doing. Jesus then asked them whether John's baptism was from God or not. Now they were trapped. If they said it was from men, the crowds would oppose them. And they did not want to say it was from God.

We see Jesus's wisdom in His silence. There were times when He said nothing. During His trial He did not try to defend Himself. He was silent. The Roman authorities were amazed. They had never seen anyone so calm. He did not have to defend Himself. What these rulers thought was weakness was the power of God. What they thought was foolishness was the wisdom of God. There are times when silence is best. Words may not be needed. Jesus knew when to speak and when to be silent.

How wisely Jesus led His disciples. They were sometimes brash and haughty. They misunderstood many things. At times they wanted to take matters into their own hands. But Jesus stood by them. He taught them patiently. He knew that they would understand in the future. He knew they would fail, but He knew that they would also become bold witnesses. Wisdom is patient, despite appearances. Wisdom looks beyond the immediate circumstances to the goal. Wisdom looks beyond where we are now to where we will be in the future.

If we could amass all the knowledge and wisdom from past ages, it would be as nothing compared to the wisdom of Jesus. He is the wisdom of God, "in whom are hidden all the treasures of wisdom and knowledge" (Colossians 2:3). In Jesus there is not part of God's wisdom, but all of His wisdom. In Christ we have all the wisdom we need for today and all we will need for tomorrow. No wonder that the writer of Proverbs says that wisdom is more valuable than silver, gold, and rubies. This wisdom comes with Jesus.

"Human language falls short of expressing all that He is, even as a thimble lacks capacity to hold Niagara Falls. The Fact of facts, the Bible's theme—He stands alone, august, unique, supreme. All comparisons, all similes, all metaphors but skirt the edges of the glory of this matchless person in whom all sanctities and sufferings unite."[28] These words from R. G. Lee express what we must say when we consider any part of Jesus's life. He always goes beyond what we can think or say. He is matchless in His wisdom.

CHAPTER 14

THERE'S NO ONE LIKE JESUS IN HIS RICHES

THE FORBES LIST DOCUMENTS THE wealthiest people in the world. According to this list, there are more than 1,500 people from different countries who own between 1 billion dollars and 76 billion dollars. There are 50 people who have 17 billion dollars or more. I do not question the accuracy of this listing, but should there not be another person at the head of the list?

The One of whom I speak owns all things. He owns all material things and all spiritual things. His name is Jesus. He owns everything! Paul proclaimed "the unsearchable riches of Christ" (Ephesians 3:8b). In this same book, Paul speaks about the "riches of His grace" and the "riches of His glory"(Ephesians 2:7; 3:16 NKJV). "In whom are hidden all the treasures of wisdom and knowledge" (Colossians 2:3). In Hebrews 1:2, it says that Jesus was "appointed heir of all things." The richest person in the created universe has incalculable riches.

What would you do if you received word that someone had opened an account in your name for 100 million dollars? No doubt you would be greatly surprised. You would go to the bank and investigate whether it was true or not. If you were convinced that it was true, you could write a check for anything that you wanted or needed. If you wanted a new car, it would be no problem: you would simply write a check. If you wanted to pay off your home loan, all you would have to do would be to write a check. It would be yours to use freely. However, if you were reckless with your spending, even such a large sum of money would sooner or later be exhausted.

Christians, though, can never use up our heavenly bank account in Christ. When we receive some blessing or experience more of His grace, there is no less that we can receive. We cannot use up the spiritual riches we have in Christ. Paul calls them "unsearchable." They are no less real than the material riches of men. What are these riches? They are anything that we need. There are no qualifiers or limits concerning these riches. They are all in Christ. It can best be put this way: our riches are Jesus Himself. To have Him is to have everything we have ever needed, everything we could possibly need, and everything that we will need in the future. In Christ, the supply always far exceeds the demand.

An Indian pastor who is also a leper reportedly said, "Jesus is all I need, Jesus is all I have, Jesus is all I want."[29] In a very old book written by Richard and Joseph Alleine, there is this insightful statement: "Christian, get to know your God, for the more you know the more you will have."[30] The more we know about Christ, the more we will know what we have. St. Augustine once suggested a way that a person could know whether he had true faith or not. (I am paraphrasing what he said.) "If God told you that you could have anything that you wanted including lands, riches, or any conceivable thing, but you could not see His face, what would you choose? If you turned down everything and chose to see His face, you are a true believer." Christ is true riches.

The riches of Christ are always beneficial. To win a lottery often brings unimaginable problems. Riches can be used to destroy. They can also become a god that people worship. The riches of Christ always lift the one who receives them. They always point to the Benefactor. Jesus used His riches to redeem and to save. They are riches of grace, which we need every day. They are riches of glory that we will one day experience more fully. Jesus comes with His riches. We do not separate Him from faith, because He is the object of our faith. We do not separate Him from love or hope. They come with Him.

Some riches take flight and are soon gone. The riches of Christ are lasting. The gifts that He gives out of His riches are lasting: love, joy, peace, patience, kindness, goodness, faithfulness, gentleness, and self-control (Galatians 5:22-23). Paul pointed out that nothing can separate us from the love of God in Christ: nothing seen or unseen and nothing in the present or in the future. "For I am convinced that neither death nor life, neither angels nor demons, neither the present nor the future, nor any powers, neither height nor depth, nor anything else in all creation, will be able to separate us from the love of God that is in Christ Jesus our Lord" (Romans 8:38–39).

Christ's riches are extravagant. We see this in nature. There are so many stars that we cannot count them. The same is true concerning birds, animals, and plant life. There is a super-abundance. This is also true in the spiritual realm. Jesus gives life, but it is abundant life. He gives life with Him now but also life in the future with Him. Paul said that His grace "super-abounded." He uses that same word *super* to describe many of the blessings that we have in Christ.

The riches of Jesus are accessible. They are accessible all the time. What good will money do you, if you do not have access to the account? The Bible makes it clear that Christ is near us. He is with us. There are never any recorded messages telling us to call back later or leave a number. There is never any word from our Lord saying that He does not have time or is too busy. In the very moment we call out, He is available.

Jesus never lacks resources to help us. There is never a famine in His mercies. We need never worry about asking for too much. He has more than we could ever think about asking. This anonymous poem appeared in a daily devotional booklet.

All I need He will always be,

All I need till His face I see,

All I need through eternity,

Jesus is all I need.[31]

In reality, our names should be added to the list of the wealthiest people. Christians are called "joint-heirs with Christ." In other words, all that Christ inherits He gives to us. He distributes His wealth, but not in small chunks. He gives everything to us, not just part of Himself, but all that He is; not just part of His righteousness, but all of His righteousness; not just part of His love, but He gives all His love. We will be welcomed and treated as Jesus, the Son of God. We are accepted in the Beloved and all His riches are credited to us. These incalculable riches cause us to lift our voices in praise to the One who became poor in order that we could be rich.

CHAPTER 15

THERE'S NO ONE LIKE JESUS IN HIS FREEDOM

SIMON BOLIVAR FREED SEVERAL COUNTRIES in Latin America from the rule of Spain. Alexander the Liberator freed the serfs in Russia. Nelson Mandela was considered to be the modern liberator in his country. In American history Abraham Lincoln freed the slaves through the Emancipation Proclamation in 1863. Millions of people enjoy freedom today because of these courageous leaders.

Moses was certainly a liberator when he led the children of Israel out of the Egyptian bondage. Esther is another liberator who spoke up when it could have meant her death. Through her action many people were freed from impending death. All these liberators were great. But excelling them all as a liberator is Jesus. Wherever Jesus goes, there is freedom. Jesus said, "Then you will know the truth, and the truth will set you free" (John 8:32). He further explained what He meant by saying, "So if the Son sets you free, you will be free indeed" (John 8:36).

What is the freedom that Jesus gives? It is the freedom to be what God meant us to be. It is the freedom not to be controlled by what other people think. It is the freedom to enjoy all the benefits of a citizen of heaven. It is the freedom to make wise choices in the light of God's will. It is the freedom of children living under the care of their Heavenly Father.

Freedom is costly. Many soldiers have given their lives in order that this country could be free. The freedom that Jesus gives is also very costly. In fact, never has there been a greater cost than what was paid for our freedom. In His death on the cross, Jesus paid the ultimate price. The Bible calls this payment *redemption*. Jesus went into the slave market and purchased slaves of sin through His death. It was not through paying silver or gold but through His death that He makes us free.

At the beginning of His ministry, Jesus went into the synagogue. He read these words from the book of Isaiah: "The Spirit of the Lord is on Me, because He has anointed Me to preach good news to the poor. He has sent Me to proclaim freedom for the prisoners" (Luke 4:18a). These words tell what His mission was. He came to free the prisoners. He has the keys to the prison. The door is now open. Why then would anyone choose to stay in the prison? Some people stay in self-made prisons. Some stay in prisons that others have built around them. What are those prisons?

They are the lies that people believe. Jesus is the truth to bring us out of the prison.

Homeless people will sometimes deliberately commit crimes so they can go to a prison, because there they will have a warm place to sleep and food to eat. Jesus is the home where we will find true freedom. He said, "I am the truth." Light is a symbol for truth. The light of Christ will shine into our dark prisons so we can step into freedom.

Political freedom may be very fragile. It can be taken away by the whims of a dictator. But in the freedom of Jesus, there is security. It is a freedom that no one can take from us. The reason is that we are in Christ. Before someone could get to us, they would have to go through Jesus. Jesus Himself is our safety. We are as secure as He is secure.

One of the main ideas of the book of Galatians is our freedom in Christ. Paul warns that we should not let the teaching or pressures of other people disturb our freedom. "It is for freedom that Christ has set us free. Stand firm, then, and do not let yourselves be burdened again by a yoke of slavery" (Galatians 5:1). How big is the freedom of Christ? It is as big as His love, as big as His will, and as big as His purpose for us.

Freedom in Christ is much like the freedom in a family. Family members are not in shackles. But parents set out guidelines. They point out dangers. They may even discipline, but this is all done in love. We are in the family of God. Our Father and Elder Brother give us guidelines. They point out dangers and will sometimes even discipline us.

John Newton experienced the freedom of Christ in profound ways. He had once been a virtual slave aboard a slave ship. When he met Christ, though, he was freed from his life of debauchery and sin. Then he could not help but write about the amazing grace of God.

In *Pilgrim's Progress* John Bunyan describes the trials of a Christian in the journey of life. He shows what happens when Christians deviate from the narrow road: there will be temporary enslavements. The wonderful thing about our freedom in Christ, though, is that we have One who will walk with us. Not only does He free us, but He also gives us direction and strength to enjoy His freedom.

Freedom in Christ excels all other freedom. It will never lead to another dark prison. Always there will be freedom before us, until one day we reach home and we can say, "Free at last." Christ comes not to impose freedom upon us but to give us a freedom that we have longed for throughout our lives. Paul thought he was free as he faithfully followed the prescribed religious laws. The surprise came when he met Jesus, and his values were then turned upside down. What he once had thought to be freedom, he now saw to be only bondage. He was made free. He wrote, "Now the Lord is the Spirit, and where the Spirit of the Lord is, there is freedom" (2 Corinthians 3:17).

There is no one like Jesus in the freedom that He gives. It is freedom that leads straight to the throne of God. It is freedom in which we will grow spiritually and call others into His freedom. No one can break the shackles of sin like Jesus. No one can open the prison doors like Him. He is the Great Liberator indeed.

CHAPTER 16

THERE'S NO ONE LIKE JESUS IN HIS RULE

SUCCESSION IS A MARK OF earthly kings. One succeeds another. It is often a matter of family relations. The eldest son follows his father. But history often gives examples of kings who took the position by force; they seized the throne by military might.

There have been many different kinds of kings. Some were despots who ruled harshly, to the detriment of the citizens. Some were limited in power. Today many kings or queens are mere titular positions. They are symbols of the state and often appear as representatives of their country.

Jesus is different from any of the kings mentioned above. Jesus did not become a king. He has always been a king. Even as a tiny baby in the manger, He was King. He was King as He walked the dusty roads of Judea and Galilee. He was King when He was tried before Pilate. He was King when He hung on the cross between two thieves. The word, *king*, was used to describe God in the Old Testament. Psalm 24 speaks of the Lord as "the King of glory." Isaiah's prophecy spoke of the coming Messiah as a king: "And the government will be on His shoulders" (Isaiah 9:6a).

Some kings have ruled for long periods of time. King David ruled for 40 years, but there was an insurrection and an attempted overthrow by one of his sons. Solomon, who followed David, ruled for 40 years, but his kingdom was divided. In secular history Louis XIV ruled for 72 years in France. France became a very powerful country during that time, but their king also died. Queen Victoria ruled for 67 years in the United Kingdom and one-fourth of the earth was under her rule. But like others before her, she passed from the scene by death.

Change marks the rule of earthly monarchs. Sooner or later they are gone and their rule ends. The rule of Jesus is changeless. Men may fight against Him. Nations may rail against Him. But they only hurt themselves. His rule is unending. There are no successors. "Of the increase of His government and peace there will be no end. He will reign on David's throne and over his kingdom, establishing and upholding it with justice and righteousness from that time on and forever. The zeal of the Lord Almighty will accomplish this" (Isaiah 9:7). No betrayals, no wars, no unbelief, and no power will change His rule.

Pilate asked Jesus whether He was a king or not. "Jesus answered 'You are right in saying I am a king. In fact, for this reason

I was born, and for this I came into the world, to testify to the truth. Everyone on the side of truth listens to me'" (John 18:37b). Jesus was different from all other kings that Pilate knew about. Pilate was puzzled, because a king has a kingdom but he could not see Jesus's kingdom. How could He then be a king? Jesus said, "My kingdom is not of this world. If it were, my servants would fight to prevent my arrest by the Jews. But now my kingdom is from another place" (John 18:36).

Wherever Jesus is, there is the kingdom. The kingdom is His rule. There is an invisible aspect to the kingdom and an outward aspect. Jesus said that the kingdom is within us; He rules in our hearts. But one day the outward aspect of the kingdom will be manifested. Jesus will return as the King of Glory. And His rule shall be forever.

The rule of Christ is done in righteousness and justice. Our King never winks at sin and injustice. He never dismisses rebellion against God. This is the reason that our King ruled from the cross. The King took the sins of the world upon Himself. The King rose from the grave. Our King provides the righteousness that we can never attain in ourselves.

In the book of Revelation we read about the King upon His throne. There the redeemed cast their crowns before the throne. There is only One who is worthy of all worship, adoration, and praise. He is the King of Kings. Not just a king, but He is above all kings.

Some kings are powerless to carry out helpful programs for their people. This may be because of a lack of resources or a lack of authority. But our King has both. He has the power and He has the resources. This is stated beautifully in Daniel's vision: "In my vision at night I looked, and there before me was one like a son of man, coming with the clouds of heaven. He approached the Ancient of Days and was led into His presence. He was given authority, glory and sovereign power; all peoples, nations and men of every language worshiped Him. His dominion is an everlasting dominion that will not pass away, and His kingdom is one that will never be destroyed" (Daniel 7:13–14).

No king has ever humbled himself like our King. Jesus laid aside the robes of glory to take on human flesh. He left a royal palace of love to come to a hate-filled ghetto. Not only did He come to us, but He also lived among us. He experienced rejection. He suffered many indignities in His death. The crowds cried out, "Crucify Him, crucify Him." Soldiers mocked Him. He wore a crown of thorns. He did all this that He might bring us into His kingdom. Is it any wonder then that every knee will bow and every tongue will confess that Jesus is Lord?

Usually, kings are known for their extravagance and their wealth. One day we will see our King in His glory. The first time Jesus came was as a servant. When He comes again, He will return as a king. He will reign forever. And our King will share all His goodness and glory with us!

CHAPTER 17

THERE'S NO ONE LIKE JESUS IN HIS JOY

UNTIL RECENT YEARS PICTURES OF Jesus usually depicted Him as very somber looking. He would look quite serious, even sad. It is true that the Bible says that Jesus was "a man of sorrows." But that does not mean that He was not also a person full of joy. The sorrows that Jesus experienced were real. He took our sorrows and entered into our sorrows. However, sorrow does not have to extinguish joy.

Several artists have painted pictures of Jesus smiling or laughing. One artist has painted a picture of Jesus dancing around with children. Bruce Marchiano made a big impact when he played the part of Christ in *The Gospel According to Matthew* in the Visual Bible series. Marchiano portrayed Jesus as laughing, smiling, and enjoying life. When Jesus healed a leper, it shows Jesus rolling in the dirt with the healed man. There was excitement as Jesus enjoyed life with His disciples. Here is what Marchiano says about his role in the movie: "With all the joy, excitement, and passion Jesus displays in Matthew, I don't think we even remotely came close! That's just how joyous, exciting, and passionate I believe Jesus truly was 2,000 years ago and truly is today."[32]

A book that influenced Marchiano's view of Jesus's joy is entitled *Jesus, Man of Joy*. In this book Sherwood E. Wirt defines joy in this way: "Joy is merriment without frivolity, hilarity without raucousness, and mirth without cruelty. Joy is sportive without being rakish and festive without being tasteless. Joy radiates animation, sparkle and buoyancy. It is more than fun, yet it has fun. It expresses itself in laughter and elation, yet it draws from a deep spring that keeps flowing long after the laughter has died and the tears have come."[33]

It should not surprise us to think of Jesus in this way. God is the source of all joy. Before the creation there was perfect joy in the Trinity. The Bible speaks of God singing. "He will take great delight in you, He will quiet you with His love, He will rejoice over you with singing" (Zephaniah 3:17b). Isaiah speaks of God rejoicing like a bridegroom over a bride. Peter J. Kreeft writes, "God is an overflowing fountain of joy, a volcanic explosion of joy, a trillion burning suns of joy, a joy that would utterly break our hearts if we touched even a drop of it at its source."[34]

What should trouble us are descriptions of a Jesus without joy. Jesus had more joy than all the world put together. He lived in joy from all eternity. He was the source of joy. Jesus occasionally spoke of His joy. In the Gospel of John there are two references. The first is John 15:11: "I have told you this so that my joy may be in you and that your joy may be complete." The second passage is John 17:13: "I am coming to you now, but I say these things while I am still in the world, so that they may have the full measure of my joy within them."

Jesus cannot give what He does not have. And joy is what He gives. Wherever Jesus is, there is joy. Jesus Himself is our joy. Joy is one of the fruits of the Spirit. "But the fruit of the Spirit is love, joy, peace, patience, kindness, goodness, faithfulness, gentleness and self-control" (Galatians 5:22-23a). All of these fruits were in perfect balance in His life. This was true throughout His life. There was no lack of any one of these fruits. Distractions and weaknesses keep things out of balance in our lives. We experience many of these fruits dimly. But that was not true with Jesus. He had joy such as no other man has ever experienced.

Jesus fully did His Father's will. There was perfect harmony between Him and His Father. Jesus was not torn by competing desires of the flesh. In Jesus we see the image of God as God planned things in the beginning. He planned for joy. And Jesus manifested joy in what He said and in what He did. There was an explosion of joy when Jesus came. That joy spread as people saw what Jesus did. There was excitement. Jesus was always surprising people. And that is what joy does. That joy even came out of an empty tomb. The words of joy were these: "He is risen."

The word *blessed* is used to speak of God. Jesus used the same word in the Beatitudes. Some translations say *happy* instead of *blessed*, and some use *blissful*. *Blessed* is a word that expresses fullness of joy, complete joy. That is what Jesus had—fullness of joy. "You have made known to me the path of life; you will fill me with joy in your presence, with eternal pleasures at your right hand" (Psalm 16:11). And where is Jesus today? He is at the right hand of the Father, where there is eternal joy.

What would attract a group of rough fishermen and cause them to leave their work to follow Jesus? Surely it would not be a condemning, sad person. No, it was the joy and the love of Jesus that acted like a magnet to draw them. What would attract little children to Him? Surely they would not be attracted to an uncaring, disinterested person. No, they were attracted to the joy and excitement of Jesus.

It is difficult for us to imagine the depths of the joy that Jesus had. But we can enter into His joy now. We can experience increasing joy through Him. And one day He will say to us, "Enter into my joy." What an inexpressible joy that will be, because it will be His joy that we enter. It is said that many martyrs faced death cheerfully. How could they do that? They knew they were going to joy, not leaving joy. The Christian lives in joy and always moves toward joy. It is the joy of a living Jesus. There's no one like Jesus when it comes to joy!

CHAPTER 18

THERE'S NO ONE LIKE JESUS IN HIS FRESHNESS

A NEW CAR, A NEW house, new clothes, and a new opportunity all appeal to people. We like new things, fresh things. Long ago, the writer of the book of Ecclesiastes asked whether there was any new thing. Whatever he tried seemed to become old. Where was something that would be fresh all the time? What he was looking for is found in the eternal Jesus. There is always a freshness, a newness in Him. In Psalm 110:3 it speaks of "the dew of your youth."

With Jesus we are always at the beginnings of our understanding, our faith, and our love. We never graduate from the school of Jesus. We are ever His disciples. Having infinite knowledge, He will show us many things that we cannot comprehend now. Jesus told His disciples that there were many things that they could not grasp now but the Holy Spirit would teach them later. There are many things that we could not understand even if we were told about them. We will never understand everything about Jesus.

Alexander Maclaren wrote, "He who has sounded the depths of Jesus most completely is ever the first to acknowledge that he has been but as a child 'gathering pebbles on the beach while the great ocean lies unsounded before him.' No single soul, and no multitude of souls, can exhaust Jesus; neither our individual experiences, nor the experiences of a believing world can fully realize the endless wealth laid up in Him."[35]

John Flavel compared our knowing Christ to someone discovering a new country. The discoverer gradually moves farther into the country. Referring to Christ, Flavel said, "The best of us are yet but upon the borders of this vast continent."[36]

Often a husband and wife seem to know each other inside and out. But occasionally, one of them will tell something utterly surprising about themselves. And the other one will say, "I didn't know that about you." As human beings, we never know another person fully. It should not surprise us, then, to know that the One who is both God and man, our Lord Jesus, will always have new things to reveal. He will never be boring. It may be boring to be around some people, but never will we feel that way about Jesus. George Morrison said that "Christ is forever young."[37]

Think of Jesus! He is eternal freshness. All of the freshness that we find in nature points to Him. There is the freshness of a flowing mountain stream. There is the freshness of the early morning when the sun first rises. There is the freshness of a fluffy snow that falls on a dark winter night. There is the freshness of the flowers that burst into color during the spring. He made all these things in the beginning, and they all point to Him who is much greater than anything He made in nature. Charles H. Spurgeon noted, "For the real Christ is always fresh, always interesting, always new."[38]

G. Campbell Morgan expressed the freshness of Christ in this way: "He is unchanged in the fact of His perpetual freshness, so that no soul has ever found it to be monotonous to walk with Him or talk with Him or think of Him or sing of Him; He is perpetually breaking in upon the soul with new surprises, in some amazing and lightning flash, or as the freshness of a morning in the springtime."[39] As an old man on the island of Patmos, John still saw the exciting newness in Jesus. What he saw amazed him and filled him with wonder!

In his book about the attributes of God, A. W. Tozer pointed out that there may be many attributes of God that we know nothing about. He refers to Frederick Faber who spoke of "the God of a thousand attributes"[40] and to one of Charles Wesley's hymns in which he uses the word *numberless* concerning the attributes of God. The One who is both God and man, Jesus Christ, has the same attributes. There will never be a graduation in our walk with Him. All that we know will fill us with joy and we will want to know more. What we know will be true, but there will always be far more that we do not know about Him.

Consider the love of Christ. We experience His love at the present time. But it is only a tiny trickle of the love that abounds in Him. His love will always be amazing us. It will always be like hearing it for the first time. There will never be an oldness to His love. Alexander Whyte wrote of Christ's love in this way: "To all eternity the love of Christ to you will be new. It will fill you full of wonder, and expectation, and imagination; full of joy and sweetness and satisfaction: and still the half will not be known to you. Heap up eternity upon eternity, and still the love of Christ to you will make all eternity to be but the springtime of life to you, and still but the early days of your everlasting espousals. The love of Christ will, absolutely and everlastingly, pass all knowledge."[41]

In John's Gospel he writes that if all the things that Christ did should be written in books, the world would not be able to contain them. Christ is such a matchless, inexhaustible person that He is always new even though He is "the same yesterday and today and forever" (Hebrews 13:8). He is changeless but not old. He is eternal but always young. It is difficult for us to understand this reality, because all around us things are always moving from youthfulness to old age, from newness to oldness, from life to death. Jesus is ultimate reality and He is the everliving One!

Because the eternal Christ is always young, we cannot help but sing, "More about Jesus would I know." It is natural for us to cry out with the Psalmist, "My soul thirsts for God, for the living God" (Psalm 42:2a). It is urgent that we proclaim the good news about Jesus who is ever our contemporary and ever new.

CHAPTER 19

THERE'S NO ONE LIKE JESUS IN HIS INFLUENCE

THE INFLUENCE OF JESUS IS ongoing. It is worldwide. There is no adequate measure of His influence. Yet there are many things we can say about His influence. He has influenced the past tremendously. All of history is marked by these letters: BC or AD, which mean "before Christ" and "after Christ." Not only did all history move toward Him, but all history since His birth also moves from Him. Jesus told His disciples to go into all the world and preach the gospel. Today you will find His followers throughout the world and sometimes in the most unexpected places.

We can see His influence in the commitment of those who follow Him. It is said that there have been more martyrs in the last century than in all previous times. What would cause people to die for Christ? It is who Jesus is and what He has done. Not only do we see His influence through martyrdom, but many of Jesus's followers also suffer unspeakable pressures and trials today.

Sometimes the persecution comes from governments. Sometimes it comes through the activities of other religions. It may even come from close family members.

Influential leaders in history pale into insignificance when compared to the influence of the Man of Galilee. In the book of Revelation, we see a picture of people coming from every tribe and people. They all bow before the throne and worship, saying, "Worthy is the Lamb." The family of Jesus comes from throughout the earth. His influence is universal in scope.

The status of women has changed because Jesus came. He elevated women. Women were often treated as second-class citizens in ancient times. What Jesus taught and did changed traditional attitudes toward women. Jesus was respectful and kind toward women as well as men. Some of His earliest followers were women.

There have been major changes in education due to the influence of Jesus. Many of the great educational institutions in the world today were begun by Christians. The principles of Jesus were incorporated into many schools. Without Jesus many colleges and universities would not exist.

Medical care and hospitals have also been impacted by Jesus. Jesus's care for the sick and needy has been the impetus for much medical service. Wherever the gospel is taken, you will find Christians who get involved in medical care. Many of the first hospitals were started by Christians. And even today many of the great hospitals are operated by churches. Jesus cared for the total man: body, mind, and soul.

I once read about a village in Romania. It was known as a very bad place. Crime was rampant. Then a Christian began to preach in the village. After some time, people began to turn to Christ. Crime ceased. The tavern closed. And the police were no longer needed. All this happened because of the living Christ.

The way that we care for prisoners and the operation of prisons have also been influenced by Jesus in amazing ways. The Olmos Prison in La Plata, Argentina, is a maximum-security prison that holds about 3,000 men. In the 1980s it was known because of the riots and danger inside the prison. All that changed, however, as the gospel was preached. There are now over 1,500 followers of Jesus inside Olmos prison. The prison has probably the world's largest prison church. Authorities have sent out some of these Christian prisoners to the other prisons of Argentina. There are now prison churches in all forty of the prisons in Argentina.

The influence of Jesus is so pervasive in the world that it is diffi-cult for us to imagine how society would be without that influence. Think of your town or city without any churches. Remove all the Christian universities and hospitals. Remove the benevolent min-istries such as the Salvation Army, the food pantries, and the meal services offered through churches. Remove all the rescue missions where the homeless find shelter. Shut down all the Christian book-stores and all the Christian radio and television broadcasts. Take away all the Christian citizens who are the salt of the earth. Take away all Christian influence from the correctional facilities. Take away any Christian influence from the military forces and from the halls of government. To imagine these things can help us to see how much of the influence of Jesus we take for granted.

Jesus's influence is not a passive thing. Wherever the followers of Christ proclaim the gospel, He is there. He speaks through us and empowers us. He invites people to follow Him through us. His influence is always benevolent. It is never coercive. His influence is through His message and what He has done. Jesus once said, "But I, when I am lifted up from the earth, will draw all men to myself" (John 12:32).

The influence of Jesus is expressed so beautifully in a well-known writing. It is sometimes attributed to "Anonymous," but it is believed to have been written by Dr. James Allen Francis in a sermon published in the early 1900s. It is called "One Solitary Life."

He was born in an obscure village

The child of a peasant woman

He grew up in another obscure village

Where He worked in a carpenter shop

Until He was thirty when public opinion turned against Him

He never wrote a book

He never held an office

He never went to college

He never visited a big city

He never traveled more than two hundred miles

From the place where He was born

He did none of the things

Usually associated with greatness

He had no credentials but Himself

He was only thirty-three

His friends ran away

One of them denied Him

He was turned over to His enemies

And went through the mockery of a trial

He was nailed to a cross between two thieves

While dying, His executioners gambled for His clothing

The only property He had on earth

When He was dead

He was laid in a borrowed grave

Through the pity of a friend

Nineteen centuries have come and gone

And today Jesus is the central figure of the human race

And the leader of mankind's progress

All the armies that have ever marched

All the navies that have ever sailed

All the parliaments that have ever sat

All the kings that ever reigned put together

Have not affected the life of mankind on earth

As powerfully as that one solitary life.[42]

CHAPTER 20

THERE'S NO ONE LIKE JESUS IN HIS RETURN

SOME FAMOUS GENERALS AND KINGS have made remarkable returns in history. King David returned after an insurrection led by his own son Absalom. After heroic battles, multitudes will sometimes shout praises to returning soldiers. What distinguishes the return of Christ is the nature and the purpose of His return. No other founder of a religion promises to return. Only Jesus said that He would return to this earth.

The first time Jesus came, He came humbly as a baby in a manger. His deity was veiled. When He comes the second time, He is coming in glory. He is coming as a King to receive His citizens. He is coming as our Elder Brother to receive His siblings. He is coming as the Mighty Conqueror to receive His soldiers. It will be a time of great victory. It will be a time of endings and beginnings. It will be a time of revealing and surprising.

Jesus spoke clearly about His future. No other prophet or teacher could speak with such certainty about the future. But Jesus not only knew what He would do in the future, but He also knew our future. Our future is all related to Him. Jesus said, "And if I go and prepare a place for you, I will come back and take you to be with Me that you also may be where I am" (John 14:3). Jesus said clearly that He would come back again. When Jesus was questioned by the high priest in a mockery of a trial and asked if He was the Messiah, Jesus answered: "I am . . . And you will see the Son of Man sitting at the right hand of the Mighty One and coming on the clouds of heaven" (Mark 14:62).

In the Bible clouds often signified the presence of God. No television coverage will be needed on the day Jesus returns to the earth. This will be a public event beyond our powers of imagination. The Bible says that the same Jesus will come again. It will not be another person. It will be the same person who is both God and man. What will be different is the fact that Jesus is coming in glory. In Titus 2:13 the second advent is called "the blessed hope—the glorious appearing of our great God and Savior, Jesus Christ." In the last book of the Bible, His Second Coming is emphasized. "Look, He is coming with the clouds, and every eye will see Him" (Revelation 1:7a).

If Jesus were not to return, it would be like having school without a graduation. It would be like having a courtship without a marriage. It would be like having a war without a victory. It would be like traveling without a destination. It would be like birth without a life. It would be like planting without a harvest. Jesus's return is just as essential as His first coming. When the fullness of time arrived the first time, Jesus came to the earth. When the fullness of time comes the second time, Jesus will return.

Without the return of Jesus, there would be many beginnings but no ending. The Alpha and the Omega will finish the work that He began. He will do this as the Judge. He is coming to make all things right. He is coming that creation can be redeemed. Paul speaks of creation groaning like a woman about to give birth. He talks about the liberation of the creation. "The creation waits in eager expectation for the sons of God to be revealed" (Romans 8:19). The reason for this waiting is given in verse 21 of the same chapter: "that the creation itself will be liberated from its bondage to decay and brought into the glorious freedom of the children of God."

The Bible teaches that all judgment has been committed to Jesus. The one offended will be the Judge. There is so much injustice in this world. The poor often suffer at the hands of the rich. The weak often are downtrodden. It would be difficult to list all the crimes that have been committed against humanity. There are also many conflicts in families and among nations. Human judgment often errs. We only see part of the picture. We can never see what is going on in a person's heart. Jesus did not need any man to teach Him, because He understood what was in the heart of man. From our perspective we cannot evaluate a person's life. Their influence goes beyond their time on earth. Only at the Second Coming can a full evaluation be made.

Jesus will do what is right. There will be a great separation based on the choice that people made during this life. Many people will go to the place they have chosen: a place of outer darkness, a place called hell, a place apart from God. Rebellion and sin will be put down. The Bible speaks of the earth burning. Whatever that may mean, we know that this earth and universe will be made new. It will experience a new birth. All things will be made new!

The followers of Jesus will be manifested. In some ways we are often hidden during this life. The judgment is not so much to determine where we go as it is to manifest who we are. John wrote that just as this world did not know Jesus, so it does not know us. But when Jesus appears, then we will be made known. John explains, "When He appears, we shall be like Him, for we shall see Him as He is" (1 John 3:2b).

When Jesus comes again, we will be with Him forever. We will be learning more and more about His greatness. We will enter into His glory. Always Jesus will be the center and focus of our lives. There will be none of the distractions that we experience here. But the Lamb will be upon His throne. And we will be with Him. That said it all for Paul: "to be with Christ." And that says it all for us as well. The return of Christ means that we will be with Him; we will be with the One we love; we will be with the One we worship; we will be with the One to whom we owe an infinite debt of gratitude.

G. Campbell Morgan wrote in one of his sermons: "We cannot exhaust Him in the human person even in the glory. He is more than a person that can be seen. That person is the revelation of the Infinite Mystery; that person is coming again to gather His people to Himself, and to be the localized King and Judge of humanity, but the infinite and the eternal and the immeasurable quantities will abide there and here."[43]

The return of Christ is not peripheral for Christian doctrine. There is no one like Jesus. And His return is absolutely essential, as is His incarnation, His death, and His resurrection. Howard A. Redmond quoted Emil Brunner as having said this: "Without the return, Christianity is a check that is never cashed, a flight of stairs that leads nowhere."[44]

What Jesus said is what no other person could say or would dare to say. He said clearly, "I am coming again." "For the Son of Man is going to come in His Father's glory with His angels, and then He will reward each person according to what he has done" (Matthew 16:27). The Second Coming is as certain and unique as was the first coming of Jesus. There will never be anyone like Jesus in His return.

THE CONCLUSION

THE GREATNESS OF JESUS FAR exceeds our ability to describe Him. We can multiply words and use countless adjectives. We can sing our best songs with the most beautiful of voices. We can paint the most imaginative pictures. All of these things together fail to express adequately the glories of Jesus. He is always above us. He is always before us as the great I Am.

There is no one like Jesus from the past. There is no one like Jesus in the present. There will be no other person like Jesus ever. He stands alone in His majesty and beauty. He is God and He is also man, forever united in one person. He is the perfect revelation of the Father. We are astounded when we see the things He did. They are unique and unequalled. Whether it is creation, salvation, or His present ministry in heaven, He amazes and surprises us.

There is no competitor in the church. He is the head, and He surpasses all our needs and expectations. From whichever perspective we look at Him in His many positions and relations, He is not just at the top of the list, but He is preeminent. He is the Lord of all.

Wherever Jesus goes, there is an unmistakable fragrance of love. There is the attraction of "an inexpressible and glorious joy." There is an assurance of the "peace of God, which transcends all understanding." There is the reality of a patience that will not let us go. We never outgrow our need for Him. We are like babies who know their mothers but who can tell so very little about them.

Charles H. Spurgeon wrote, "There is all that your soul could take in of any one thing, and more than your soul could take in if it were multiplied a million times, and could take in a million precious things at once. There is all you ever have wanted, and all you ever will want. Did I say, 'want'? There is in Christ all you can desire, for that is one of His names, 'He is all desires.'"[45]

More and more, deeper and deeper, higher and higher . . . those words express what we always experience as we follow the One before whom every knee will bow and every tongue confess that He is Lord. He alone is worthy. All that we have, all that we can do, and all that we desire comes through the grace of One who is the same yesterday and today and forever.

Samuel Rutherford seems to soar to heaven as he says, "Oh! Who can add to Him who is that great All! If He would create suns and moons, new heavens, thousand and thousand degrees more perfect than these that now are, and again, make a new creation ten thousand thousand degrees in perfection beyond that new creation; and again, still for eternity multiply new heavens, they should never be a perfect resemblance to that infinite excellence, order, weight, measure, beauty, and sweetness that is in Him."[46]

ENDNOTES

1 Samuel Rutherford, *Letters of Samuel Rutherford* (Edinburgh: Banner of Truth, 1984) 446.

2 J. Sidlow Baxter, *The Master Theme of the Bible* (Wheaton, IL: Tyndale, 1973) 181.

3 Charles H. Spurgeon, *Metropolitan Tabernacle Pulpit, Vol. 30* (Edinburgh: Banner of Truth, 1971) 28.

4 John Watson, as quoted in *The Nature and Character of God* by W. A. Pratney (Minneapolis, MN: Bethany House, 1988) 391.

5 Charles E. Jefferson, as quoted in *The Heart of the New Testament* by H. I. Hester (Nashville: B & H Academic, 1980) 7.

6 E. Stanley Jones, as quoted in *The Nature and Character of God* by W. A. Pratney (Minneapolis, MN: Bethany House, 1988) 394.

7 Colin Brown, *That You May Believe* (Grand Rapids, MI: Eerdmans, 1985) 38.

8 Erich Sauer, *The King of the Earth* (Palm Springs, CA: Ronald N. Haynes, 1981) 177, 209.

9 David Redding, *The Miracles of Christ* (Westwood, NJ: Revell, 1964) viii.

10 William Hendricks, *A Theology for Children* (Nashville: Broadman, 1980) 102.

11 C. S. Lewis, *Miracles* (New York: MacMillan, 1959) 83.

12 Phillip Schaff, *The Person of Christ* (Hannibal, MO: Granted Ministries, 2011) 82.

13 Richard A. Swenson, *More Than Meets the Eye* (Colorado Springs, CO: NavPress, 2000) 103.

14 United Airlines *Mainline* magazine, March 1978, p. 43, as quoted in Thomas Dubay, *The Evidential Power of Beauty* (San Francisco: Ignatius, 1999) 232.

15 Michael Horton, *The Gospel-Driven Life* (Grand Rapids, MI: Baker, 2009) 79.

16 Robert Lowry, *The Worship Hymnal* (Nashville: Lifeway, 2008) 223.

17 John Oxenham, *The Worship Hymnal* (Nashville: Lifeway, 2008) 394.

18 Bruce Marchiano, *Jesus* (Eugene, OR: Harvest House, 1999) 50.

19 Walter A. Elwell, ed., *Evangelical Dictionary of Theology* (Grand Rapids, MI: Baker, 1984) 1034.

20 Steve DeWitt, *Eyes Wide Open* (Grand Rapids, MI: Credo House, 2012) 48–49.

21 Charles H. Spurgeon, *Morning and Evening* (Nashville: Thomas Nelson, 1994) Feb. 8 Morning.

22 John Newton, *The Worship Hymnal* (Nashville: Lifeway, 2008) 323.

23 Erich Sauer, *In the Arena of Faith* (Grand Rapids, MI: Eerdmans, 1956) 13.

24 G. Campbell Morgan, *The Westminster Pulpit, Vol. 1* (Grand Rapids, MI: Baker, 1995) 117, 119.

25 J. Wilbur Chapman, *The Worship Hymnal* (Nashville: Lifeway, 2008) 156.

26 John Ortberg, *Who Is This Man?* (Grand Rapids, MI: Zondervan, 2012) 82.

27 Mike Nappa, *God in Slow Motion* (Nashville: Thomas Nelson, 2013) 150.

28 Robert G. Lee, *A Greater Than Solomon* (Jefferson City, MO: Le Roi Reprint, 1935) 7.

29 Joe Coffey and Bob Bevington, *Red like Blood* (Wapwallopen, PA: Shepherd, 2011) 49–50.

30 Richard and Joseph Alleine, *Heaven Opened* (NFCE Publishing, date unknown; first published in 1665) 4.

31 Anonymous, *Our Daily Bread* (date unknown).

32 Bruce Marchiano, *In the Footsteps of Jesus* (Eugene, OR: Harvest House, 1997) 79.

33 Sherwood E. Wirt, *Jesus, Man of Joy* (Eugene, OR: Harvest House, 1999) 45.

34 Peter J. Kreeft, *Everything You Ever Wanted to Know about Heaven* (San Francisco: Harper & Row, 1982) 102.

35 Alexander Maclaren, *Exposition of Holy Scripture: 2 Corinthians* (Grand Rapids, MI: Baker, 1977) 55.

36 John Flavel, *Works of John Flavel, Vol. 1* (Edinburgh: Banner of Truth, 1982) 36.

37 George H. Morrison, *Floodtide* (Grand Rapids, MI: Baker, 1971) 282.

38 Charles H. Spurgeon, *Metropolitan Tabernacle Pulpit, Vol. 47* (Pasadena, CA: Pilgrim, 1977) 204.

39 G. Campbell Morgan, *The Westminster Pulpit, Vol. 9* (Grand Rapids, MI: Baker, 1995) 68.

40 A. W. Tozer, *The Knowledge of the Holy* (New York: Harper & Row, 1961) 20–21.

41 Alexander Whyte, *Lord, Teach Us to Pray* (Grand Rapids, MI: Baker, 1976) 155.

42 John Allen Francis, *The Real Jesus and Other Sermons* (Valley Forge, PA: Judson Press, 1926). (Author sometimes listed as "'Anonymous.')"

43 G. Campbell Morgan, *The Westminster Pulpit, Vol. 6* (Grand Rapids, MI: Baker, 1995) 196.

44 Emil Brunner, as quoted in *A Philosophy of the Second Advent* by Howard A. Redmond (Fenton, MI: Mott Media, 1985) 94.

45 Charles H. Spurgeon, *Metropolitan Tabernacle Pulpit, Vol. 42* (Pasadena, CA: Pilgrim , 1976) 403.

46 Samuel Rutherford, *Letters of Samuel Rutherford* (Edinburgh: Banner of Truth, 1984) 577.

For more information about

Blake Western

&

No One Like Jesus

please visit
www.blakewestern.com
BlakeWestern37@gmail.com

For more information about
AMBASSADOR INTERNATIONAL
please visit:

www.ambassador-international.com
@AmbassadorIntl
www.facebook.com/AmbassadorIntl